Help YOUR Team

OVERCOMING COMMON COLLABORATIVE CHALLENGES IN A PLC AT WORK®

MICHAEL D. BAYEWITZ | SCOTT A. CUNNINGHAM

JOSEPH A. IANORA | BRANDON JONES | MARIA NIELSEN

WILL REMMERT | BOB SONJU | JEANNE SPILLER

FOREWORD BY **Mike Mattos**

Solution Tree | Press *a division of*
Solution Tree

555 North Morton Street
Bloomington, IN 47404
800.733.6786 (toll free) / 812.336.7700
FAX: 812.336.7790

email: info@SolutionTree.com
SolutionTree.com

Visit **go.SolutionTree.com/PLCbooks** to download the free reproducibles in this book.

Printed in the United States of America

Library of Congress Cataloging-in-Publication Data

Names: Bayewitz, Michael D., author.
Title: Help your team : overcoming common collaborative challenges in a PLC
    at Work® / Michael D. Bayewitz, Scott A. Cunningham, Joseph A. Ianora,
    Brandon Jones, Maria Nielsen, Will Remmert, Bob Sonju, Jeanne Spiller.
Description: Bloomington, IN : Solution Tree Press, [2020] | Includes
    bibliographical references and index.
Identifiers: LCCN 2019011048 | ISBN 9781947604612 (perfect bound)
Subjects: LCSH: Teaching teams. | Team learning approach in education. |
    Teachers--Professional relationships.
Classification: LCC LB1029.T4 B379 2020 | DDC 371.14/8--dc23 LC record available at
    https://lccn.loc.gov/2019011048

Solution Tree
Jeffrey C. Jones, CEO
Edmund M. Ackerman, President

Solution Tree Press
President and Publisher: Douglas M. Rife
Associate Publisher: Sarah Payne-Mills
Art Director: Rian Anderson
Managing Production Editor: Kendra Slayton
Senior Production Editor: Christine Hood
Content Development Specialist: Amy Rubenstein
Copy Editor: Miranda Addonizio
Proofreader: Jessi Finn
Editorial Assistant: Sarah Ludwig

Acknowledgments

I would like to thank my parents, Howard and Ellen Bayewitz, for being my first and finest teachers. I would also like to thank my family—Mara, Molly, Ezra, and Zoe—for their patience and love. My seven fellow coauthors are amazing educators but finer people. Thanks for teaching me and stretching me, and for your friendship, despite your horrible taste in baseball teams. Finally, this book would never have been possible without the collective impact Rick DuFour made on each of us. Rick, thank you.

—Mike Bayewitz

I would like to thank my parents, Bill and Kay, for always believing in me and instilling in me the belief that we must always be kind and caring toward others and can make a difference. I miss you, Dad, and I love you, Mom.

—Scott Cunningham

Of the many things on my bucket list, writing a book was more of a far-fetched dream than a reality. Thanks to my PLC family, and more specifically, to our wonderful sophomore cohort, who made this dream a reality. I love you guys! A special thank you to my family for their love and support!

—Joe Ianora

First and foremost, I give thanks to God, the original author and architect of all things. Without Him, none of the blessings of this book would be possible. To my loving wife, Sarah, whose support never wavers and who sacrificially cared for our family while this work was completed; I owe you the world! I dedicate my efforts in this book to my parents and my heroes, Robert and Cathy. You've imparted wisdom, perseverance, and a passion for helping others, and I am eternally grateful.

When I traveled to Indiana in 2011, I thought I was going for a job interview. I had no idea I was actually there to meet seven new best friends. Cohorts, you all have challenged and encouraged me more than you will ever know in this journey to educate all students. I am so thankful to engage in this work with such power-houses in education and to be called a member of the sophomore class of associates!

—Brandon Jones

It has been an honor writing this book with my dearest friends, the sophomore class of associates. Everyone has freely brought his or her gifts and expertise to the table. Thank you for inspiring me, making me belly laugh at group texts, and changing the lives of the students we serve every day. Thanks also to my husband, Clayton, and to my children for their love and support in this important work.

—Maria Nielsen

The 2012 cohort of Solution Tree Associates has been the best model of collabora-tion in my professional life. I appreciate every one of you and how you've pushed and supported me to heights I didn't know I was capable of reaching. A heartfelt thank you to my children, Charlie, Grace, and Emmy, and parents, Bill and Patty, for their never-ending support and love.

—Will Remmert

One of the greatest benefits to being in the world of education is the many people you meet each day who assist your growth as an educator and person. My coauthors are truly some of the best! Although at times it seemed like a "rodeo" of sorts, the compilation of thoughts, ideas, and practices shared in this book are proof that true collaboration can occur with the varied perspectives, collective creativity, and unwavering commitment of passionate educators. Thanks to you all!

—Bob Sonju

This book was something we talked about after knowing each other for about two days, and I am so grateful that it is now a reality. Thank you to this amazing group of educational leaders for the opportunity to be part of a truly collaborative team focused on learning. I have learned so much from all of you and look forward to our continued friendship and collaboration. Thanks also to my family for always supporting and encouraging me in my work.

—Jeanne Spiller

Solution Tree Press would like to thank the following reviewers:

Becky Elliott
Assistant Principal
Academy of the Holy Names
Tampa, Florida

Teri Gough
Fifth-Grade Teacher
Sundance Elementary School
Los Lunas, New Mexico

Kelly Grigsby
Academic Dean
Escondido High School
Escondido, California

Liann Hanson
Principal
Oak Crest Elementary School
Belle Plaine, Minnesota

Thomas Kennedy
Principal
Rocky Mountain Middle School
Idaho Falls, Idaho

Iram Khan
Principal
McLeod Road Traditional School
Surrey, British Columbia
Canada

Visit **go.SolutionTree.com/PLCbooks** to download the free reproducibles in this book.

Table of Contents

4 Planning for Targeted and Effective Team Interventions 53

5 Working Together in a PLC 73

6 Changing to a Positive School Culture 93

7 Involving Nondepartmental Members in a PLC . . . 105

8 Supporting Singleton Teachers in Collaborative Teams 123

About the Authors

Michael D. Bayewitz is currently the proud principal of Cloverly Elementary School in Silver Spring, Maryland. He has also previously served as a director of elementary schools, principal, assistant principal, and classroom teacher. Through his twenty-five years of education experience, he has provided supervision and direct support to over seventy schools at the elementary, middle, and high school level.

From 2007 to 2012, Michael served as principal of Broad Acres Elementary School in Silver Spring, Maryland. Through the building of a professional learning community (PLC), Broad Acres gained national attention for its dramatic increases in student achievement. At the elementary school, 95 percent of students receive free and reduced-price meals—the highest percentage in the district—and 70 percent of the students are English learners. In the year 2000, less than 20 percent of students passed state exams. With a collaborative culture, targeted interventions, and a unique strategy for parent engagement, student achievement improved. By 2012, Broad Acres reached 88 percent proficiency in reading and 95 percent in mathematics on the Maryland State Assessment.

Michael received the 2011 Dr. Edward Shirley Award for excellence in educational administration and supervision. He earned a dual bachelor's degree in political science and African American and African studies from Binghamton University. He earned a master's degree in elementary education from George Washington University and received an administrative certification from Johns Hopkins University.

To learn more about Michael Bayewitz's work, follow him @mbayewitz on Twitter.

Scott A. Cunningham is principal of Orange Middle School (Olentangy Local School District) in Ohio. He has more than twenty-three years of experience in education as a principal, assistant principal, and teacher. As principal of Norton Middle School in Columbus, Ohio, Scott and his team transformed this low-achieving school into a nationally recognized model PLC.

With a poverty rate of more than 75 percent and a diverse population of students from more than twenty different countries, Norton earned an excellent rating from the Ohio Department of Education, making adequate yearly progress in all areas and demonstrating above-average growth in value-added data (top 15 percent in the state).

Scott holds a bachelor of science in biology from Ohio Northern University and a master of education in curriculum and instruction from Ashland University.

Joseph A. Ianora has spent sixteen of his thirty-two years (1999–2015) in education as an administrator. He has been both a comprehensive and continuation high school principal. Prior to that, he held nearly every position in a school site, including custodian, counselor, teacher, campus minister, coach, and 504 coordinator. Joe uses his varied school experiences to help transform schools into 21st century, student-centered learning facilities.

Joe began his career at an all-boys high school in New York. He moved to California, where he continued his teaching and counseling career, working with inner-city students. He became principal of San Ramon Valley High School in 2004. As principal, Joe worked with his staff as a PLC for eight years. Under his leadership, this school was consistently named a top-performing school by *U.S. News and World Report* and a California Distinguished School in 2006, 2009, and 2012. In 2012, it was ranked eighty-eighth out of 2,200 schools in California for its academic program and student engagement. In 2012, Joe moved into alternative education and used the tenets of the PLC process to increase his school's graduation rate from 72 percent to 89 percent, with a forty-five-point API increase.

He received an undergraduate degree in philosophy, psychology, and theology, and a master of arts in counseling from Saint Mary's College of California. He holds a pupil personnel services credential and an administrative services credential. Joe is also a certified educational coach and a licensed marriage and family therapist.

To learn more about Joseph A. Ianora's work, follow him @jianora on Twitter or on Facebook.

Brandon Jones is an author and consultant and works with educators of all grade levels to develop and enhance teacher leadership, build sustainable collaborative teams, and produce effective systems for a tiered approach to response to intervention (RTI) using the PLC at Work® and RTI at Work™ processes.

As a principal of elementary, middle, and high school campuses in Texas, Brandon helped lead cultural and systemic change processes that have resulted in exceptional student achievement. His campuses have been recognized at the state and national levels for outstanding student achievement, progressive learning practices, and systems of intervention that ensure success for every student.

Brandon holds a bachelor's degree in science education from East Texas Baptist University and a master's degree in educational leadership from Stephen F. Austin State University.

To learn more about Brandon Jones's work, follow him @1DrivenByVision on Twitter.

Maria Nielsen, consultant and author, specializes in supporting teachers and administrators in the areas of PLC at Work, RTI at Work, transforming school culture, curriculum design, the highly engaged classroom, and assessment systems. Her passion is helping schools build successful systems to ensure high levels of student learning.

Maria has more than thirty-five years' experience as a teacher and administrator at the elementary, middle, and high school levels in Utah. As a principal, Maria helped Millville Elementary earn state and national recognition as a high-progress, high-achievement Title I school. Solution Tree named the school a national model PLC in 2012.

Maria was named the 2007 Utah Behavior Initiatives Principal of the Year. In 2010, she received the distinguished Huntsman Award for Excellence in Education.

She holds a bachelor's degree in education from Utah State University, a master of science in education from Utah State University, and an administrative endorsement from Idaho State University.

To learn more about Maria Nielsen's work, follow her @marianielsenplc on Twitter.

Will Remmert is an elementary principal and consultant and holds a doctorate in organizational leadership, policy, and development from the University of Minnesota. He works with educators at all levels to implement proven practices designed to enhance student and professional learning through the PLC at Work and RTI at Work processes.

With more than twenty years of experience as a teacher and administrator at both the elementary and secondary levels, Will has been instrumental in leading his staff to adopt a collaborative culture focused on improving student learning for all. His work led Washington Elementary to be recognized by AllThingsPLC (www.allthingsplc.info) as a model PLC school, as well as earning the unique distinction of Reward School by the Minnesota Department of Education for ranking in the top 15 percent of Title I schools in the state.

Will's doctoral work focuses on the impact of school culture, professional community, leadership, and belief ideologies for improved student learning. He holds an undergraduate degree in elementary education from Minnesota State University, Mankato and a master's degree and an administrative degree from Saint Mary's University of Minnesota.

To learn more about Will Remmert's work, follow him @willremmert on Twitter.

Bob Sonju is an award-winning educational leader, author, and consultant recognized for his energetic commitment to building effective teams, developing RTI structures that support teachers and students, and creating an effective school culture committed to learning for all students. He was also the executive director of teaching and learning for Washington County School District. After six years as a district-level administrator, Bob's deep desire to work with teachers and students again led him back to school as principal of Washington Fields Intermediate.

Bob was formerly the principal of Fossil Ridge Intermediate School and has also served as a high school administrator and special education teacher. While leading Fossil Ridge Intermediate, Bob and his staff developed a true PLC that continues to produce extraordinary results. In 2013 and 2016, Fossil Ridge received the prestigious National Breakthrough School Award by the National Association of Secondary School Principals. Fossil Ridge continues to be listed as a national model PLC and has been featured in *Principal Leadership* magazine and on AllThingsPLC (www.allthingsplc.info). As a district leader, Bob led the implementation of the PLC process in a district composed of fifty schools.

The Utah Association of Secondary School Principals named Bob 2011 Principal of the Year for middle-level schools, and the National Association of Secondary School Principals selected him as one of three finalists for National Principal of the Year. His work has been published in *Principal Leadership* magazine; *It's About Time, Secondary*; and *Best Practices at Tier 2, Secondary*.

Bob earned a bachelor's degree, a master's degree, and an endorsement in school administration from Southern Utah University.

Jeanne Spiller is assistant superintendent for teaching and learning for Kildeer Countryside Community Consolidated School District 96 in Buffalo Grove, Illinois. School District 96 is recognized on AllThingsPLC (www.allthingsplc.info) as one of only a small number of school districts with all schools in the district earning the distinction of model PLC. Jeanne's work focuses on standards-aligned instruction and assessment practices. She supports schools and districts across the United States to gain clarity about and implement the four critical questions of a PLC. She is passionate about collaborating with schools to develop systems for teaching and learning that keep the focus on student results and helping teachers determine how to approach instruction so that all students learn at high levels.

Jeanne received a 2014 Illinois Those Who Excel Award for significant contributions to the state's public and nonpublic elementary schools in administration. She is a graduate of the 2008 Learning Forward Academy, where she learned how to plan and implement professional learning that improves educator practice and increases student achievement. She has served as a classroom teacher, team leader, middle school administrator, and director of professional learning. Jeanne earned a master's degree in educational teaching and leadership from Saint Xavier University, a master's degree in educational administration from Loyola University Chicago, and an educational administrative superintendent endorsement from Northern Illinois University.

To learn more about Jeanne Spiller's work, visit www.livingtheplclife.com or follow her @jeeneemarie on Twitter.

To book Michael D. Bayewitz, Scott A. Cunningham, Joseph A. Ianora, Brandon Jones, Maria Nielsen, Will Remmert, Bob Sonju, or Jeanne Spiller for professional development, contact pd@SolutionTree.com.

Foreword:
The Inherent Dichotomy of Teamwork

By Mike Mattos

Who doesn't like the idea of being part of a team? This means working together to achieve a greater goal; building the deep bonds of cooperation and teamwork; knowing that when you stumble, your teammates have your back; benefiting from the collective talents of every member; and being part of something bigger than yourself. Like the 1980 U.S. men's Olympic hockey team, or the NASA team that successfully guided the ill-fated Apollo 13 astronauts back home, a true team can achieve results that are impossible to reach alone—accomplishments that are professionally profound and personally rewarding.

Unfortunately, this idealistic vision of teamwork often fades when one actually begins to work closely with colleagues. Sometimes the team's mission is unclear, and the greater goal dissolves into competing personal agendas. Individual team members' strengths are replaced by annoying colleague idiosyncrasies. Instead of having your back, a teammate "stabs" you there. Your collective efforts resemble a dogsled: a few doing all the pulling, while someone stands in the back and goes along for the ride. Dissent, distrust, and disillusionment weaken the contributions of each team member and leave frustrated individuals longing for the days of mildly effective isolation.

In education, teachers face this inherent dichotomy of teamwork. At a time when schools must ensure every student succeeds, it's unrealistic to expect educators to achieve this goal by working in isolation. Securing high levels of learning for every student requires highly effective teamwork. Specifically, the world's best-performing school systems achieve this level of collaboration by functioning as professional learning communities (PLCs; Barber, Chijioke, & Mourshed, 2010; Barber & Mourshed, 2007).

Equally important, this collaboration must focus on the outcomes that most positively impact student learning. Ronald Gallimore, Bradley Ermeling, William Saunders, and Claude Goldenberg (2009) find that "to be successful, teams need to set and share goals to work on that are immediately applicable to their classrooms. Without such goals, teams will drift toward superficial discussions and truncated efforts" (p. 548). The four critical questions of a PLC at Work® capture these goals (DuFour, DuFour, Eaker, Many, & Mattos, 2016).

1. What do students need to know and be able to do?

2. How will we know if they learned it?

3. How will we respond if they don't learn it?

4. How will we extend the learning for those who know it?

Digging deeply into these four questions will directly and significantly impact classroom instruction, assessment, intervention, and extension practices—and subsequently improve student learning. That is, it will if the individuals collaborating together can come together to truly be a team.

My Experience With Teacher Teams

From 2001 to 2009, I had the privilege of serving as principal at two schools that strived to become a PLC, specifically committing to the PLC at Work framework that was first developed by Dr. Richard DuFour and Dr. Robert Eaker (1998). Collaborative teacher teams are the engines that drive the PLC at Work process. When these teams are highly engaged in the right work, student learning accelerates forward . . . and when they are not, learning sputters and stalls.

The faculties at each school quickly embraced the potential benefits of collaboration, for both students and educators. Working with the teachers' union, we scheduled weekly time for job-alike teacher teams to work together—time that did not require the faculty to work beyond their existing contractual day. Additionally, we used faculty meeting time to clarify the essential work of each team and determine the resources necessary to successfully complete each task. With these prerequisite conditions in place, we were ready—actually excited—to begin reaping the fruits of our collective efforts. We quickly learned that true teamwork is easy to embrace but much harder to actually achieve.

Some teams struggled to bind together the unique working styles of each member. For example, one team had some members who wanted to monitor team meeting time carefully, allocating predetermined blocks of time for each topic and having a teammate serve as the time monitor to ensure the team followed the agenda. But other teammates found this format much too rigid, potentially stymieing creativity and the free-flowing exchange of ideas. Another team had some members who wanted to start each meeting with a check-in when team members would share how they were feeling. Other members felt this touchy-feely activity was unnecessary and wasted precious work time.

These disagreements might seem relatively minor, but they created significant team conflict and frustration. One would think that the most challenging part of a long hike is the large mountain you must climb, but instead it is often the small pebble in your shoe. Subsequently, many teachers faced with this inevitable friction saw their team progress slow to a painful crawl.

Other teams had difficulty with the essential work required to answer the four critical questions that guide team collaboration (DuFour et al., 2016). While we had consensus on the right work, some team members had never prioritized or unpacked standards. Others had no significant training on writing common formative assessments or what to do with assessment data once the test was administered. Many team members felt uncomfortable sharing their classroom assessment results with teammates and even more reticent to share their students for interventions. And almost every team found it difficult to come to consensus on what was essential for students to learn, when to teach these standards, how to assess them, and the best way to intervene. Disagreement is inevitable—and essential—in a successful PLC. If teammates can't productively turn these different perspectives into a collective path forward, the team becomes paralyzed, and the gears of collaboration grind to a halt.

Unfortunately, a few team members challenged the need to collaborate at all and purposefully sabotaged their teams. Some undermined the team through passive-resistant behaviors, such as coming to meetings late or grading papers during team discussions. Others worked stealthily behind the scenes, spreading gossip and mistrust about team members. And some just blatantly refused to do the work. Such actions would make team meetings so toxic it became nearly impossible to gain anything positive from the experience. At this point, not only did the gears of teamwork stop, but members also started to abandon ship.

And quite honestly, many of my leadership decisions were lacking, especially at the first school. While I had spent most of my career as a classroom teacher, I never worked at a school that functioned as a PLC, so I had little working knowledge of the process. I struggled to find the best teaming structures for singleton teachers and certificated support staff. The site leadership team expected teachers to work as a high-performing team but did not hold the same expectations for its members. Part of me thought I should directly supervise team meetings, while another part of me thought that the teams had to figure it out for themselves.

Looking back, I should not have been surprised by these obstacles. Most of our staff members were accustomed to working in isolation, rarely having to adjust their daily classroom practices to the collective will of their teammates. While working in isolation is not the best way to ensure all students learn, it is usually a more efficient way to get work done. The skills and behaviors required to be a good teammate are not genetic but instead develop through careful consideration, dedication, and reflection.

Considering that the origins of our profession began with an individual teacher leading a one-room schoolhouse, working closely with colleagues has not always been a professional expectation. Finally, we were not asking teachers to discuss trivial topics and complete mundane tasks. Instead, they were discussing important topics that composed the essence of their individual and collective work and would impact their students for years to come. With so much at stake, it made sense that individuals advocated passionately for their suggestions, positions, and beliefs.

While Richard DuFour ultimately named both schools as model PLCs, and the schools achieved record levels of student achievement, our journey to secure the proven benefits of collaboration was much more challenging than we originally anticipated.

Since leaving my principalship, I have had the honor to train and coach thousands of educators on the PLC at Work framework and found the challenges our teams faced were not rare, but instead the norm. I am convinced that these challenges are unavoidable, because they represent the inherent dichotomy of teaming. Deep levels of collaboration are inspiring and frustrating, empowering and demanding. If your school claims to be a PLC but does not face these challenges, then you probably aren't really doing the right work at a deep level. If you face these challenges but don't successfully overcome them, then your students will never gain the powerful benefits that collaboration can achieve. Needless to say, I was a markedly more effective leader at supporting teacher teams at the second school due to the lessons I learned the first time around. Now imagine if you had an expert to help you through these unavoidable team struggles. With this book, you have eight such experienced professionals who will help guide you.

The Benefits of Others' Experiences

Oscar Wilde (BrainyQuote, n.d.) once said, "Experience is simply the name we give our mistakes." The authors of this book—Michael Bayewitz, Scott Cunningham, Joseph Ianora, Brandon Jones, Maria Nielsen, Will Remmert, Bob Sonju, and Jeanne Spiller—have gained the depth of knowledge that can only be acquired through the experiences of doing the work. They have personally led schools and districts that are model PLCs, stretching from California to Maryland and Ohio to Texas. Additionally, they have trained, coached, and supported schools around the world. I have worked with each of them—all are exceptional educators, colleagues, and people.

Together, the authors have practiced what they preach. They have worked collaboratively to identify the most frequent, challenging obstacles that teams face when they function within a PLC. For each hurdle, they have provided research-based actions to ensure team success. Their suggestions are clear, practical, and proven. This book should serve as an ongoing resource to support school leaders and team members, as they will face different challenges throughout the journey of becoming a high-performing team.

Finally, I hope my candid portrayal of the trials of teaming does not lessen your enthusiasm or your commitment to working in teams and becoming a PLC. Consider for a moment this question: Have you ever achieved anything truly special in your life—personally or professionally—that did not first require deep levels of commitment, effort, and potential sacrifice? It would be naïve to think you can profit from teaming without a substantial investment in the process. Undoubtedly, the inherent obstacles of teaming are significant, but the benefits can be life-altering. This was true for the U.S. men's Olympic hockey team in 1980, it was true for the NASA team that safely guided a broken spacecraft back to earth, and it can be true for any team of educators truly committed to every student's success. Good luck!

Introduction

Educators have the tremendous responsibility of preparing our future generations. They can most effectively accomplish this task by collaboratively working in teams to ensure high levels of learning for all students. The collective journey isn't a simple step-by-step procedure; rather, it is an exciting, challenging, highly rewarding, and worthwhile experience as greater numbers of students bring their dreams within reach while teachers experience continuous professional learning throughout their careers.

The Purpose of This Book

This book focuses on the work of collaborative teams in a professional learning community (PLC). Its purpose is simple: to give teacher teams a resource for solving common challenges that arise during the collaboration process. Our goal is to bring together our varying experiences and perspectives to develop a practical and valuable resource for educators around the world. We were energized by the idea of sharing proven strategies and targeted tactics we've learned along the way that will assist collaborative teams to overcome many of the problems they face.

As we processed the thought of developing this book together, we were struck by the fact that we would face some of the same challenges collaborative teams face in schools! These included, but were not limited to, honoring differing perspectives, overcoming cross-country communication, and considering varied education styles. Experiencing these trials while writing the book only strengthened our resolve that this was a worthwhile venture!

We decided that we would not only share strategies and processes to help teams overcome common team challenges; we would also model some of these strategies as we compiled the elements of this book. Essentially, we would not just "talk the talk" but "walk the walk" as we found ways to collaborate, communicate, and in the end, come to consensus on the essential elements of this book. Much like a collaborative team, we developed norms, held frequent collaborative meetings, and reached consensus in a variety of target areas. It was a refreshing learning process for all of us. In the end, we functioned as a collaborative team of authors working interdependently toward a common goal to which we held one another mutually accountable—the development of this book.

In our collective experience of teams pursuing high levels of learning for every student, team members will inevitably run into challenges that, more often than not, are frustrating to their work and progress. These common team challenges are predictable, as the majority of teams face them sometime during their collective, collaborative work. With help from teachers and teams across the United States, we have identified these predictable challenges and questions. When they are resolved, rising above these trials helps teams make the most progress toward ensuring that all students learn at high levels.

In These Pages

Each chapter addresses common team concerns and questions, along with a variety of ideas, templates, processes, and strategies to help teams get unstuck.

The structure of each chapter follows a similar format.

- A short but familiar scenario describing the common team challenge the chapter will address (School and staff names are fictional and used for reader context. We developed these scenarios from frequently asked questions we have received throughout our careers as educators and educational consultants.)

- What the experts say about this challenge

- Common questions along with targeted answers, proven strategies, and various process templates to help teams solve the challenge

- Ideas for coaching teams through these strategies and practices (In this book, *coach* refers to any stakeholder who is encountering challenges and seeking a solution.)

- Additional help from proven outside resources

Chapter 1 discusses how to organize your school into the most effective types of teams. Chapter 2 addresses the challenging questions of how to manage team members who disengage from or disrupt the process, while chapter 3 discusses how teams can determine what students should know and be able to do. Chapter 4 offers readers strategies for planning targeted, effective team interventions based on the response to intervention (RTI) process. Chapter 5 describes how collaborative teams can work together effectively in a PLC, while chapter 6 helps you learn how to transform your school culture to one that is positive and supportive. Chapters 7 and 8 focus on how to include both nondepartmental staff members and singleton teachers in collaborative teams in a PLC. Finally, the epilogue concludes the book by offering cautions for collaborative teams, strategies for working through team conflicts, and ideas and actions teams must commit to in order to be highly effective.

We are excited to share these tips and tools with full confidence that, when implemented, they will give your team the skills necessary to solve common team challenges. As we begin this important journey to be the best we can be for the students we serve, the work starts when you become a member of a collaborative teacher team, which we discuss in chapter 1.

Organizing Schools Into Effective Collaborative Teams

Professional learning communities recognize that until members of the organization "do" differently, there is no reason to anticipate different results.

—Richard DuFour, Rebecca DuFour,
Robert Eaker, and Thomas W. Many

The Story of Brownsville Middle School

Brownsville Middle School has always been considered a school that is "good enough." Although its performance indicators have remained stagnant over many years, infrequent feedback surveys indicate that the community seems fairly satisfied with the school. The school routinely marginalizes or simply dismisses any constructive or critical feedback it receives from the community.

The staff at Brownsville Middle School work hard but seem to be content with maintaining the status quo. A good portion of the staff remain committed to practices they have used since their early days of teaching and often demonstrate a passive resistance to any new professional learning. The teachers are a diligent, committed group of professionals with a focus on one thing: delivering curriculum. Simply stated, this philosophy drives the general belief of the school: an underlying sense of urgency to deliver the mountain of standards it is responsible for, combined with the feeling that "it's our job to teach and the students' job to learn." Because of this, the typical cycle of instruction in most classrooms at Brownsville Middle School is simple.

- Decide what to teach.

- Teach it.

- Give an assessment.

- Place the results in the gradebook.

For students at the school, it is survival of the fittest; keep up with the frenetic pace of the content being delivered and get your work turned in on time. If you do this, you will be successful. If you don't grasp a concept or skill, the classroom teacher does his or her very best to help you understand it. But in the end, teachers just don't have the time to spend, as they have to move forward in order to keep up with the established pacing guide to meet the overwhelming number of standards they need to teach.

The leadership team and staff have varying degrees of understanding regarding the PLC process. Teachers are loosely organized into teams, with a directive from the leadership team to "go and collaborate." Teachers meet weekly during their dedicated collaboration time, and more often than not, focus their efforts on the calendar of upcoming events and sharing stories from the classroom. A few of the staff have been to a PLC institute and often returned to the school inspired with new ideas and fresh practices. But questions and doubts from the rest of the school quickly consume these ideas. Interestingly, the staff recognize that they are losing some students to their frenzied instructional pace and feel the need to make sure each student in the school learns at high levels. But they have an unclear understanding of what they are supposed to do to meet the needs of every student; doing this seems overwhelming and nearly impossible. As a result, the staff stick with what is comfortable to them and what they have always done. But educators throughout the building feel familiar unrest lying just beneath the surface; they know they need to do better.

Like many schools, Brownsville is staffed with hardworking, well-intentioned educators with varying levels of understanding about processes and practices that positively impact student learning. Some have a foundational understanding of teamwork, while others are simply familiar with the practices of collaboration, essential standards, and intervention. With the lack of clarity and understanding of practices that truly impact student learning, Brownsville Middle School's leaders and staff do their best with the sporadic, fragmented knowledge they have. As is often the case, team collaboration tends to default to discussing the calendar, reviewing untargeted assessment data, and providing generalized interventions that simply focus on the completion of work.

Some elements of the Brownsville Middle School practices should be celebrated. The staff are a diligent, committed group of professionals who have explored the PLC process and recognized that some of their students are not gaining the skills needed to be successful. Most important, the staff feel a sense of unrest; they know there is a problem but are not quite sure how to change.

As practitioners, we understand and have personal experience with this, as all of us are leading or have led schools similar to Brownsville. In this chapter and throughout this book, we have identified common team and school challenges and provide a variety of practical solutions and resources to help your team and school in their journey.

What the Experts Say

Highly successful schools, districts, and organizations share one thing in common: they are driven by a clear, compelling purpose to improve. In our collective work with educators around the world, the overwhelming majority of teachers chose the teaching profession for the purpose of making a difference in the lives of young people. This purpose compels extraordinary teachers in the United States to spend hours well beyond their contractual time, and personal resources above their meager teachers' budgets, while oftentimes sacrificing time with family and friends as they prepare to meet the varied, diverse needs of their students.

Organizational process expert Jim Collins (2001) characterizes the critical nature of being driven by something greater than oneself:

> When [what you are deeply passionate about, what you can be best in the world at, and what drives your economic engine] come together, not only does your work move toward greatness, but so does your life. For, in the end, it is impossible to have a great life unless it is a meaningful life. And it is very difficult to have a meaningful life without meaningful work. Perhaps, then, you might gain that rare tranquility that comes from knowing that you've had a hand in creating something of intrinsic excellence that makes a contribution. Indeed, you might even gain that deepest of all satisfactions: knowing that your short time here on this earth has been well spent, and that it mattered. (p. 210)

As the complexities of preparing students for a future beyond school continue to evolve, teachers feel the daunting challenge of delivering overwhelming amounts of curriculum, addressing students' ever-increasing social and emotional needs, and meeting a variety of oftentimes misguided mandates and legislation. It's easy to see why teachers can feel swamped.

For schools and districts that function as PLCs, their purpose is clear: to *ensure* that *every* student learns at high levels. This clear, compelling purpose represents more than just scoring above the designated proficiency mark on an end-of-level state exam. Instead, it's ensuring that every student in a school or district has the necessary skills to be a successful, contributing member in the changing global economy and community. But how do we accomplish this? Certainly not by teaching in isolation or focusing on just *my students*. Instead, it requires the collective efforts of teams of teachers, utilizing their collective strengths, to ensure all students, *our* students, learn at high levels.

Consider for a moment this question: Is there an educator in the world who possesses all the skills and abilities needed to meet the unique and diverse needs of every student in his or her class?

If we disagree with this statement, then this represents a real dilemma: an individual teacher doesn't possess all the skills necessary to meet the diverse needs of every student in his or her class, and yet the purpose of schools and districts that function as a PLC is to ensure that every student learns at high levels. In order to accomplish this, teachers need to organize into highly effective collaborative teams that share a common purpose and utilize the strengths of each teacher on the team to promote student learning. This collective approach to learning is reaffirmed in *Learning by Doing* by Richard DuFour, Rebecca DuFour, Robert Eaker, Thomas W. Many, and Mike Mattos (2016): "Teachers should be organized into structures that allow them to engage in meaningful collaboration that is beneficial to them and their students" (p. 64). This common purpose and these shared strengths help teachers take on the nearly impossible task of ensuring that each student learns at high levels.

John Hattie's (2016) research affirms this collective approach as he lists "collective teacher efficacy" as one of the most highly influential practices on student learning. Simply put, collective teacher efficacy is the team members' confidence in each other's abilities and their shared belief in the impact of the team's work on student learning. These key elements are what set successful teams apart. "Success lies in the critical nature of collaboration and the strength of believing that together, administrators, faculty, and students can accomplish great things. This is the power of collective efficacy" (Donohoo, Hattie, & Eells, 2018, p. 44). Thus, a school should organize its teachers into highly effective collaborative teams that are confident in and utilize each team member's strengths with the belief that their collective work will positively impact student learning.

As teams are organized and the work begins, inevitably, challenges will arise within the team. These challenges are the focus of this book, along with proven strategies, processes, and templates to help your team move forward.

Common Questions About Collaborative Teams

Following are the answers to common questions teams will inevitably face regarding organizing, selecting, collaborating with, and monitoring the work of teams in your school.

What Are the Most Effective Types of Teams?

There are a variety of ways for schools to organize educators into collaborative teams. It's important to keep in mind this key question: Which structure will help us utilize the strengths of the team and help us ensure that every student learns at high levels? If schools use this foundational question as a touchstone, then they will be able to select which structure best suits them. Possible team structures are as follows (DuFour et al., 2016).

- **Content-specific teams:** These teams consist of teachers who teach the same course or grade level (for example, the third-grade team or the language arts 10 team). This structure appears to be the most practical among larger schools with multiple teachers teaching the same subject.

- **Vertical content teams:** These teams consist of teachers who teach the same content over different grade levels (for example, a language arts team comprising the kindergarten, first-grade, and second-grade teachers in a school). This structure is especially useful for small schools that likely only have one teacher per subject.

- **Interdisciplinary teams:** These teams consist of teachers who share common students across different content areas (for example, a sixth-grade team could consist of a mathematics teacher, a science teacher, and a language arts teacher who share the same students, allowing them to find common themes and skills in their content that cut across all three curriculum areas).

- **Logical connections:** These teams consist of teachers who are pursuing the same learning outcomes (for example, teachers in special education or specialist subjects such as music, art, and physical education).

- **District or regional teams:** These teams consist of teachers who want to align outcomes across an entire district or region (for example, the district's secondary band teachers).

- **Digital content teams:** These teams consist of teachers who seek connections with colleagues across the district, state, or world (for example, music or drama teachers). This team structure is especially useful for teachers who are the only ones to teach a subject in a school (often referred to as *singletons*). Teachers on a digital team can select from a myriad of available digital platforms (for example, Google Hangouts or GoToMeeting) to collaborate.

What Work Should Teams Focus On?

Teams should focus on the fundamental purpose of a PLC: ensuring high levels of learning for every student. They can accomplish this using the four critical questions of a PLC as a framework, as DuFour et al. (2016) outline. These questions guide a team's work and help it maintain a focus on elements that achieve its purpose.

1. What do students need to know and be able to do?

2. How will we know if they learned it?

3. How will we respond if they don't learn it?

4. How will we extend the learning for those who know it?

Although these questions seem easy to answer, there is much more depth to each question than first appears. Each question requires teams to engage in deep conversations and specific actions in order to adequately address it. Figure 1.1 provides detailed work that teams must engage in to address each of the four critical questions of a PLC.

Following each question in the figure are steps that the team must engage in to specifically address the critical question. For example, in order for teams to gain clarity for critical question 1 (What do students need to know and be able to do?), teams must accomplish the following three steps.

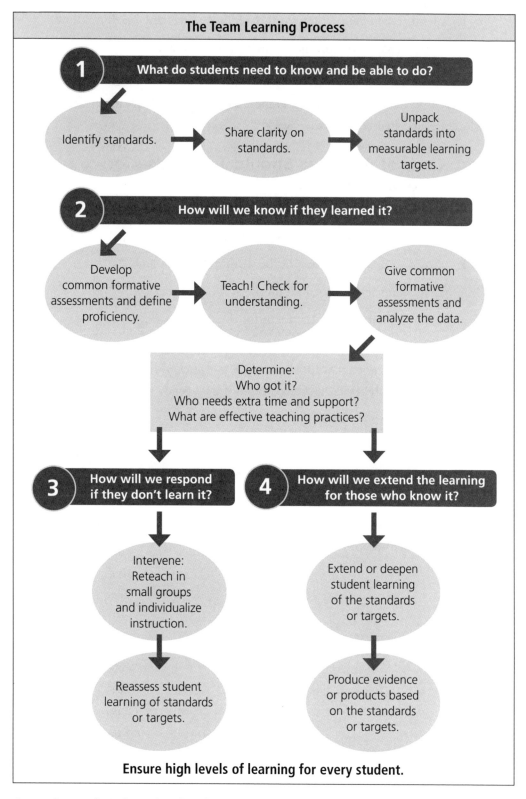

The Team Learning Process

1 What do students need to know and be able to do?

Identify standards. → Share clarity on standards. → Unpack standards into measurable learning targets.

2 How will we know if they learned it?

Develop common formative assessments and define proficiency. → Teach! Check for understanding. → Give common formative assessments and analyze the data.

Determine:
Who got it?
Who needs extra time and support?
What are effective teaching practices?

3 How will we respond if they don't learn it?

4 How will we extend the learning for those who know it?

Intervene: Reteach in small groups and individualize instruction.

Extend or deepen student learning of the standards or targets.

Reassess student learning of standards or targets.

Produce evidence or products based on the standards or targets.

Ensure high levels of learning for every student.

Source: © 2017 by Rich Smith. Adapted with permission.

Figure 1.1: The team learning process.

1. Identify the essential standards or skills that students need to know.

2. Gain shared clarity on the essential standards or skills.

3. Unpack the essential standards or skills into measurable learning targets.

Teams can use the content of this graphic to help guide their conversations and clearly articulate their collaborative work.

What Kinds of Agendas Should Teams Use for Collaborative Meetings?

Team agendas are critical to the work of teams during their collaborative meetings. These meetings should accomplish three clear goals.

1. Provide a detailed outline of the work to be completed.

2. Help teams remain focused on the work at hand.

3. Serve as a reference of the focus for the team's work.

There are a variety of team agendas schools can use, and it is important to find one that helps the team accomplish its work and meets the expectations of the school. Foundationally speaking, the content of the agenda should focus on:

•   Student learning for all

•   The four critical questions of a PLC

•   The work that the team needs to complete

Figure 1.2 and figure 1.3 (page 14) are two examples of team agendas collaborative teams can use to guide their work. (Note that the four critical questions of a PLC are embedded in both agendas.)

Heritage Team Collaborative Agenda
2018–2019

Grade-Level Team:		Date:	
Quick Coordination (Calendar items, common lessons, celebrations) Five minutes or less			

Essential Standard What are we working on teaching our students right now?	
Best Practice What will we do to make sure our students learn? Remember, high-quality core instruction should allow for about 75 percent of students to master the essential standard.	
Common Formative Assessment (CFA) How will we know when our students have learned or mastered the guaranteed and viable curriculum? Identify which teaching practices were most effective.	
Intervention Strategies What will our team collectively do for those students who didn't learn or master the guaranteed and viable curriculum identified by the common formative assessment? What is our plan to help those students master this guaranteed and viable curriculum?	
Extensions How will we challenge and extend the learning for students who have already learned or mastered the guaranteed and viable curriculum?	
What We Need Resources requested or help that the administrative team can provide, or anything else	

Source: © 2018 by Heritage Elementary School. Used with permission.

Figure 1.2: Example team agenda—Heritage Elementary School.

*Visit **go.SolutionTree.com/PLCbooks** for a free reproducible version of this figure.*

Brownsboro High School
Collaborative Team Agenda

Team		Date	
Norms			
Purpose			
Q1: What do students need to know and be able to do?		Q3: How will we respond if they don't learn it?	
Q2: How will we know if they learned it?		Q4: How will we extend the learning for those who know it?	
☐ Q1—Essential standards ☐ Q2—To what depth or rigor ☐ Q2—Classroom quick checks ☐ Q2—Common formative assessment ☐ Q2—Curriculum-based assessment		☐ Q2—Midterm or final exam ☐ Q2—Data (programmatic and best practices) ☐ Q2—Data (individual students) ☐ Q3—Intervening and remediating ☐ Q4—Extending and enriching	
Outcomes and Products			
☐ Q1		☐ Q2	
☐ Q3		☐ Q4	
Questions or Follow-Up Items			

Source: © 2018 by Brandon Jones, Brownsboro High School. Used with permission.

Figure 1.3: Example team agenda—Brownsboro High School.

*Visit **go.SolutionTree.com/PLCbooks** for a free reproducible version of this figure.*

How Can Teams Monitor Their Progress for Doing the Right Work?

Strong, highly impactful teams are willing to take a critical look at themselves in order to improve their collective effectiveness in meeting the needs of all students.

Oftentimes, in the busyness of the school year, even the best teams can drift away from focusing on their purpose. It's critical for teams to check their progress often in fundamental areas. The rubric in figure 1.4 can serve as a monthly touchstone for teams to frequently check their progress and effectiveness as a team. When used effectively, it provides the context for targeted conversations and plans to help teams move forward.

Key Considerations: Effective Teams	Embedded	Developing	Emerging	No Evidence
Essential standards: Our team has come to consensus and shared clarity on the essential standards and skills that all students need to know and be able to do.				
Common formative assessments: Our team utilizes common formative assessments to determine which students have met agreed-on proficiency goals and which need extra time and support.				
Time and support: Our team responds immediately to students who need extra time and support to master an essential standard or skill.				
Intervention: Our team's interventions are immediate, specific, and targeted.				
Collaboration: Our collaborative meetings are focused on learning, individual students, learning data, and intervention or extensions.				

Figure 1.4: Effective teams rubric.

*Visit **go.SolutionTree.com/PLCbooks** for a free reproducible version of this figure.*

Have teams follow these directions to use the rubric in figure 1.4.

1. Have each team member complete the rubric by reading the indicator on the left and marking where he or she currently sees the team.

    ○ **Embedded:** We do this without even thinking about it; it's part of how we do business.

    ○ **Developing:** We understand it, and for the most part, we do it. But it takes a little work to stay on course.

    ○ **Emerging:** Some of our team members do, and some don't. We are a little fragmented in this area.

    ○ **No evidence:** We seem to struggle in this area.

2. Once done, team members get together to share their rubrics and discuss why they marked each section the way they did.

3. Following discussion, team members come to consensus on an area of strength and an area of challenge.

4. The team then identifies next steps to commit to moving forward.

How to Coach Your Team

Organizing your school into effective teams is a critical first step for schools desiring to improve their collective effectiveness. As you consider the collaborative team and structure that would best work for the teachers in your school, consider the following three questions to help you organize teachers into meaningful teams.

1. Are there teachers on staff who teach in the same content areas and share the same curriculum? (Consider a content team.)

2. Are there teachers who are the only ones to teach in a content area—for example, one first-grade teacher, one second-grade teacher, and so on? (Consider a vertical team.)

3. Are there teachers who are the only ones to teach a specialized content area in the school—for example, the only family and consumer science teacher? (Consider a digital team.)

When building and developing effective teams, it's important to be mindful that the connections with the teachers' collaborative team need to be relevant for them and for accomplishing the purpose of ensuring that each student on their team learns at high levels.

Conclusion

Whether on the competitive field or in the school, highly effective teams are essential for organizations to accomplish their goals. Once schools begin to organize themselves into meaningful collaborative teams, it's critical that these teams begin to learn together about the processes that truly make a difference in student learning, utilize agendas to help keep their valuable collaboration time focused and productive, and continually evaluate the effectiveness of the team's practices. This team approach to shared learning with the belief that team members' collective efforts will make a difference is the foundation for changes in practice and increases in learning that help diminish the unrest that Brownsville Middle School feels and possibly your school feels as well.

Additional Resources

Teams can use these helpful resources to gain further guidance and insights for their collaborative work.

- *The Five Dysfunctions of a Team* (pp. 191–194): Author Patrick Lencioni (2002) offers a useful assessment tool that can assist teams in avoiding what he refers to as the "five dysfunctions of a team."

- *Taking Action: A Handbook for RTI at Work* (pp. 58–61): This section of the book by Austin Buffum, Mike Mattos, and Janet Malone (2018) assists schools as they form collaborative teams and provides additional descriptions of different teams, as well as a clear, compelling case for the need for teams.

- *Learning by Doing: A Handbook for Professional Learning Communities at Work* (3rd ed.; pp. 63–67): Rich with resources, this book by DuFour et al. (2016) shares a variety of activities, action plans, and surveys to assist teams in their development and direction.

Managing Team Members
Who Disengage

*Coming together is a beginning. Keeping together
is progress. Working together is success.*

—Henry Ford

The Story of J. Howard Elementary School

At J. Howard Elementary School, the second-grade collaborative team boasts the most experience in teaching on campus. It is highly revered by peers and the community for its longevity. In fact, several of the team members have taught multiple generations of students through the years. To the team's credit, the on-grade-level and above-grade-level students traditionally perform well on their reading, writing, and mathematics assessments. However, students who enter second grade below grade level typically do not perform well. Unfortunately, the gap in learning tends to grow wider for these students as the year progresses.

In an effort to increase student achievement, the leadership team proposes that all grade-level teams determine essential standards for each content area. Its reasoning is to focus the efforts of each teacher and student around central, critical concepts and skills. Doing so would allow each team to spend less time and resources on concepts that leaders deem less important, thereby ensuring that students learn the standards they identify as essential.

All teams at the school engage in the work before the school year begins. However, the second-grade team experiences many difficulties. One team member argues the scope and sequence the team created four years ago at the staff retreat was working "just fine" for most students. Another member arrives at meetings with papers to grade and completely disengages from the conversation. A third member points out that the teachers must, by law, cover the state and national standards and any deviation from the set curriculum would create inequity between what they teach and what other elementary schools in the state teach. These team members' actions delay the process into the second quarter of the school year.

Amy, the team leader, trains everyone on the essential standards process, helps develop norms for working together, and individually meets with team members who seem to need additional information or encouragement in moving forward. Despite the fact that most teams on campus identify their essential standards and start to break them down into learning targets, the second-grade team essentially abandons the work. The idea of creating essential standards causes dissent among the team and even catches the attention of the other staff at J. Howard Elementary School. Amy requests that an administrator attend the next team meeting to assist with the conversation and offer support.

Unfortunately, scenarios like the one at J. Howard Elementary School are all too common in schools. Instead of focusing their work on best practices proven to boost student achievement, team members sometimes choose to return to isolation and the status quo, and otherwise give up on the right work. In this chapter, we provide strategies for working with team members who choose to disengage from the collaborative team process.

What the Experts Say

To establish a foundation for effective teamwork, team members must ensure that they work interdependently to achieve common goals for which they are mutually accountable (DuFour et al., 2016). Teams are more than a loose collection of people assembled to have conversations about their students or curriculum. They must center the common goals they establish on ensuring high levels of learning for all students, and achieve them through routine analysis of the four critical questions for learning (DuFour et al., 2016).

1. **What do students need to know and be able to do?** This question focuses on establishing a guaranteed and viable curriculum for all students. Teams reflect and come to a consensus on the standards for learning that are essential for each student to learn in any course, content area, or grade level.

2. **How will we know if they learned it?** This question focuses on assessing for learning. Teams make decisions and commit to the type of assessment necessary to determine if students have learned. In addition, teams review information collected from these assessments to answer questions 3 and 4.

3. **How will we respond if they don't learn it?** This question helps teams devise a plan for students who need additional time and support. Teams implement best practices in instruction as they create plans for intervention and remediation.

4. **How will we extend the learning for those who know it?** This question helps teams create a plan for students who have already mastered the required content. Teams implement best practices in instruction as they create plans for enrichment and extension.

Teams establish interdependency when they understand that no one member of the team can effectively meet the needs of all students in his or her care. We need all team members to work in unison toward this purpose. Otherwise, we are relegated to be an average school that meets the needs of some students rather than a great school that meets the needs of all.

Evidence to support this type of collaborative structure in schools exists across the globe. Marc Tucker (2015) notes:

> Teachers spend about a quarter of their time working collaboratively with one another, rather than facing students in the classroom. In the best of these systems, all teachers, except those at the top of the career ladder, have mentors. In many countries, among them Japan, mainland China, Hong Kong, and Singapore, teachers meet frequently, often weekly, by grade and by subject taught. Teachers in the upper ranks of the career ladder put teams of teachers together and lead them. These teams analyze the data on student performance, figure out what's working and what's not, determine what priorities they want to work on, do extensive research about the issue, develop new

units of curriculum or new approaches to instruction on the basis of the research, and build prototypes of the new approaches. (p. 70)

Despite mountains of clear evidence to support the collaborative process, most schools across the United States have yet to fully commit to this type of environment. Fred Newmann (1996) writes:

Comprehensive restructuring typically includes such features as site-based management, with meaningful authority over staffing, program, and budget; shared decision making; staff teams, with frequent common planning time and shared responsibility for student instruction, multi-year instructional or advisory groups, and heterogeneous grouping in core subjects. It is estimated that less than 10% of U.S. public schools are comprehensively restructured. (p. 7)

Collaborative teacher teams are designed to create interdependent relationships that promote ongoing improvement and increase effectiveness across classrooms. Despite such promise and efforts by many to create teams, most schools are not organized so teachers can collaborate regularly and intensively. Also, as Michael Huberman (1993) suggests, it may be unrealistic to expect teachers to engage with teams because interdependence takes up time and runs counter to professional norms of autonomy, judgment, and privacy that have long defined teachers' work.

Why do we bring this research to your attention? If you are facing challenges with getting all team members to engage in the collaborative process, you should know that you are not alone. We are fighting an uphill battle that has raged for decades in the public school system. The presumption and design for isolationism is prevalent and widespread in most schools today. With that said, this is also a message of hope. We can—we must—create a collaborative culture in our schools that is so prevalent and foundational that nothing will be able to stop it. In the words of Malcolm Gladwell (2002), "What must underlie [successful epidemics], in the end, is a bedrock belief that change is possible, that people can radically transform their behavior or beliefs in the face of the right kind of impetus" (p. 258).

Common Questions About Team Members Who Disengage

Following are the answers to some common questions teams might ask regarding how to deal with team members who disengage from and disrupt the collaborative process.

What Signs Should We Look for in Team Members Who Disengage?

In their book *Pyramid Response to Intervention*, Austin Buffum, Mike Mattos, and Chris Weber (2009) describe two types of students who are not learning: (1) the failed learner and (2) the intentional nonlearner. Failed learners are those who need additional time and support because they do not know how to do the work. They gave the effort and attempted to learn but have yet to demonstrate proficiency. In this case, the school has not yet provided effective instruction to meet their needs. In contrast, intentional nonlearners have chosen to opt out of the learning process. It's not that the initial instruction was not appropriate or sufficient; rather, these learners did not put forth the effort needed to master new skills. Buffum et al. (2009) state that the type of support that each learner receives must match the cause of the deficiency. For instance, a failed learner may need differentiated instruction, assistance with prerequisite skills, or simply more time to master the concepts. In contrast, the intentional nonlearner may need frequent checks for progress or required changes to his or her behavioral habits.

We would surmise you have, from time to time, run across the same types of challenges with adult learners in your team. There are those who lack the skill or prior knowledge necessary to be a contributing team member. These team members tend to have a favorable attitude toward the work and simply need more information or training to embrace the PLC process. There are also those who lack the will to collaborate with others. These team members may need an entirely different kind of support and encouragement.

To begin, let's take a look at the profile of an adult nonlearner.

We have someone on our team who:

- **Does not contribute to the work**—This team member is content with attending team meetings and sitting idly by while others engage in the work of ensuring high levels of learning for all. The extent of his or her participation is a well-timed nod to signify, at best, passive agreement with the immediate plan taking place.

- **Is routinely unprepared**—This team member views a collaborative meeting as a time to visit and catch up on the latest stories circulating on the campus rather than a time to collaborate.

- **Does not honor team norms**—This team member most likely recognizes the value in the collaborative process but does not recognize common, professional courtesies other team members have extended to one another.

- **Disengages by completing other tasks during team meetings**—This team member is most likely breaking a team norm but does so in a way that is openly brash toward other team members. He or she often tries to excuse these actions by completing otherwise legitimate tasks such as grading papers or preparing a classroom activity.

- **Wants to lead . . . all the time**—This team member deeply values the collaborative team because it gives him or her a platform to be in charge. Typically, all is well until the will of the team is different from the will of this person.

- **Pretends to engage but privately derails team efforts**—This team member uses passive-aggressive measures, such as procrastinating, expressing sullenness, or acting stubborn, to undermine the work of the team. He or she can be difficult to identify with because his or her attitude and surface-level engagement appear to be positive and supportive.

- **Actively rejects the PLC mindset, ideas, and culture**—This team member makes no effort to engage in the collaborative process. He or she supports the overall autonomy of teachers rather than the collective effort of a team. In addition, this person engages in practices and procedures that back up his or her belief in the impossibility of universal achievement for all. These actions may include, but are not limited to, engaging in antiquated grading practices, declining to give additional support to students in need, or refusing to implement instructional practices that are proven to improve student achievement.

Who Is Responsible for Addressing Team Issues?

Chances are, if you have engaged in the collaborative process for any length of time, you have experienced one or more of the previous situations. Because collaboration is so critical to the mission of high levels of learning for all, educators working in a PLC must hold each other accountable for staying focused on work aligned to that purpose. In addition, leaders must not turn a blind eye to these challenges: "Nothing will destroy the credibility of a leader faster than an unwillingness to address an obvious violation of what the organization contends is vital" (DuFour et al., 2016, p. 213).

The vast majority of businesses, governmental agencies, and schools rely on a vertical accountability system. That is, if someone in the organization deviates from or does not live up to what the culture expects, other members of the organization expect that a supervisor will step in and rectify the situation. This type of accountability continues to move up the chain of command (vertically) until the person achieves the desired outcome or behavior.

Unlike in this traditional system of accountability, a leader and team member in a PLC must engage in horizontal, or mutual, accountability. In this structure, the immediate reaction is not to look to a hierarchy of positional leadership to intervene but, rather, to rely initially on peer-to-peer interaction. For many readers, the thought of holding peers accountable for their actions is chilling. It is, understandably, more comfortable and safe to simply wait for the wheels of the traditional vertical accountability system to begin turning. But what if the wheels never turn? Or what if the conversation misses the mark because the supervisor was not directly involved in the team issue? The rest of this chapter provides tips, guidelines, and resources to help teams along this journey. They will find solutions at the team level that have the greatest and most positive impact in moving forward.

Levels of Team Accountability

There are three levels of accountability: (1) horizontal, or team; (2) mutual, or individual; and (3) vertical, or supervisor. This system provides teams with a way to hold members accountable according to agreed-on norms and values.

Level 1: Horizontal Accountability (Team)

To establish horizontal accountability, a team must first define the standards of behavior for how team members will work together. We call these standards of behavior *norms*. Teams typically establish norms of acceptable behaviors at team meetings, but norms really apply to all interactions in which teams engage. For example, if team members agree that they must positively frame all conversations about students, they should apply this to conversations in the teachers' lounge, in the hallways, and so on. In addition, teams must establish how they will handle violations of team norms. We have worked with many teams through the years that skip this critical step in the process. They use statements such as the following.

- "We're all professionals, and we know how to act."
- "We've worked together for years, so we understand the expectations of the others on our team."
- "I don't feel comfortable holding other adults accountable for how they act."

While these are common reasons for not engaging in the norms process, agreeing on simple standards for how we will treat one another while we work together is the first step to becoming a high-functioning team. Norms provide clarity and consistency when working together and, more important, necessary guideposts if and when someone begins to act in a way that is detrimental to the team.

When developing team norms, consider the following two questions.

1. What behaviors do you value when working with other people?
2. What behaviors are pet peeves when working with other people?

Compare answers to questions 1 and 2 with fellow team members. Note the behaviors team members mention frequently. These behaviors should be the basis for your team norms. Next, have team members do the following.

- Write a positive expectation statement for each of the most commonly mentioned behaviors.
- Decide how they will hold one another accountable should a team member violate the norms.

For example, a team might address norm violations by knocking on the table. If someone notices that a team member is disengaged from the conversation, he or she simply knocks on the table, reminding all team members to check that their behavior is in line with the established norms.

In addition to establishing norms, team members should agree on overarching values or collective commitments to govern team members' actions and decisions in all other facets of the school. Just as norms guide actions during team meetings, collective commitments guide behaviors and decision making in all other facets of the team that occur outside of team meetings. Creating these standards together ensures consistency within the team as each member carries out his or her particular responsibilities throughout the week, month, and year. Also, like norms, collective commitments are behaviors rather than simple beliefs.

Areas in which teams may consider acquiring consensus include, but are not limited to:

- Student learning
- Educator learning
- Collaborative culture
- Results or goals
- Assessment and grading
- Classwork and homework
- Best practices in instruction
- Celebration of progress

A school may also choose to establish collective commitments as a staff. If not, we highly encourage teams to engage in this dialogue prior to beginning the school year. The following is an example of the collective commitments from Brownsboro High School in Texas:

- We will hold one another mutually accountable for a culture that is relationship driven, caring, supportive, takes risks, and ensures ALL students learn at HIGH levels.

- We commit to implement best practices in the classroom while making student-centered, data-driven, and research-based decisions.

- We commit to collaborate with colleagues to ensure equity in education; that is, ALL students learning at HIGH levels.

- We commit to model excellence in learning by being willing, reflective and open-minded in actively improving as educators.

- We commit to promote pride in our students, school and profession by seeking success, whether big or small, to celebrate. (Brandon Jones, personal communication, August 10, 2018)

Clarifying team members' expectations before engaging in collaborative work will enhance each member's ability to contribute meaningfully to the process. These norms also provide tangible guideposts for members to use to direct their efforts.

Level 2: Mutual Accountability (Individual)

Horizontal team accountability provides a solid foundation from which to work. However, despite clear expectations and whole-group reminders, some individuals may continue to disengage from or even derail the team process. When this occurs, the team leader must address the behavior directly. Many team leaders consider this the most difficult function they perform. To be fair, no university offers a class for aspiring teachers called Holding Colleagues Accountable 101! With that in mind, here are a few helpful tips to remember when the time comes for that conversation.

- Enter the conversation with the expectation that this person is trying to do his or her very best for students.

- Focus on the behavior or processes lacking, not the person.

- Tie each expectation back to the pre-established norms or commitments.

- Collaborate on measurable improvements or adjustments in behavior.

- Resist the temptation to gloss over or sugarcoat the issue. Be collegial and empathetic, and address each issue that needs to improve.

For leaders who may be new to this process, the following conversation stems may be helpful to engage with colleagues.

- "Thank you for taking a few minutes to visit with me about your role in our collaborative team. I'd like to begin by thanking you for . . ." (*Focus on a positive contribution that your colleague makes to the team or to the students you serve.*)

- "With that (*positive contribution*) in mind, how do you feel you best support the mission of our team to help all students learn at high levels?"

- "Now I'd like to review the norms or commitments we made to one another earlier in the year . . ." (*Have a copy for each of you and read them together.*)

- "Just to review, these standards of behavior are critically important for each of us to uphold because . . ." (*Explain why you developed these norms or commitments and the negative impact it has on the team or students when someone breaks one or more of them.*)

- "Of these norms, I have noticed you are excellent in upholding (*a few, some, most, almost all*) of them, but there is (*one, a few, several*) behavior that has become routine over the last several weeks. While I appreciate the effort being made toward (*the norms that are being upheld*), I'd like to focus the remainder of our conversation on (*the norm that is being consistently broken*)."

- "Here are a few specific examples of when this norm was broken in recent weeks."

- "Would you like to respond to these behaviors I have mentioned?"

- "To make our team the best it can be, in moving forward, we need . . ." (*Give specific expectations for behavior related to the norms or commitments being broken.*)

- "Do you have any clarifying questions about what to expect as we move forward?"

- "I will help support you with this change by . . ." (*Explain how you will provide support and continued accountability in the near future.*)

- "Thank you again for visiting with me. I look forward to strengthening our collaboration together as we reach our goals as a team."

When done well and with the right intentions, this type of peer-to-peer conversation is highly effective in changing desired behaviors. In the days and weeks that follow, continue to monitor actions and celebrate improvements toward the team's norms and commitments. A little encouragement helps perpetuate continued growth and progress.

Another element to consider when faced with this type of conversation is when to inform campus administration of the concern. In most cases, administrators will want to know details surrounding the issue and when the matter became significant enough to warrant being addressed by a team member. They may be able to offer further guidance or insight into the upcoming conversation. However, do not ask or expect them to become personally involved at this juncture. Doing so would skip this incredibly important step of exercising mutual accountability within the team structure. While we acknowledge this part of the process is difficult for some teacher leaders, take courage from the fact that it's an opportunity to make a positive impact on student learning and the professional life of a colleague. Consider the words of Kerry Patterson, Joseph Grenny, David Maxfield, Ron McMillan, and Al Switzler (2008):

> The point isn't that people need to be threatened to perform. The
> point is that if you are unwilling to go to the mat when people violate

a core value (such as giving their best effort), that value loses its moral force in the organization. On the other hand, you send a powerful message about your values when you hold people accountable. (p. 216)

Level 3: Vertical Accountability (Supervisor)

In the unlikely event a team member is still derailing or disengaging from the team process even after participating in the first two levels of accountability, the need for supervisory support is inevitable. With the support previously provided cooperatively by the team and individually by the leader, we can surmise the team member is now acting as an intentional nonlearner. He or she has the knowledge and skills necessary to fully engage with the team but lacks the will to do so. The vertical accountability that a supervisor can provide may be the encouragement this team member needs to move forward in a positive way.

When entering this stage of accountability, the team leader should provide all information to the administrator regarding the behavior in question as well as the supports the team and leader have provided. The more information the administrator has up front, the more prepared he or she will be to address the concerns.

If appropriate, the team leader should be present during the conversation with the team member. This ensures accuracy of the information given as well as a pathway for clarification, when needed.

While no one wants to have these types of interactions with a colleague, they are often necessary in organizations that aspire to go from good to great. In a PLC, our primary mission is to ensure all students learn at high levels. To reach this goal, it takes a collective effort from everyone involved in the organization. This mission and vision of what your organization can become should drive all decision-making processes and also, ultimately, supersede your desire to ensure that all adults in the organization are comfortable.

How to Coach Your Team

Coaching your team through these processes can be challenging at first. However, once you establish team norms and commitments on which everyone agrees, you have laid the foundation of clarity you need to move forward with all levels of accountability.

Level 1: Horizontal Accountability (Team)

The keys to success in this accountability level include the following five steps.

1. Establish norms and commitments before the school year begins.

2. Agree on a method all team members will use to hold one another accountable.

3. Remind everyone of the norms and commitments regularly, preferably at each team meeting.

4. Routinely hold one another accountable using the agreed-on informal method.

5. Review the norms and commitments you have made to one another one to two times per year. Make revisions, as needed, to ensure the behavioral guidelines are continuing to meet the needs of the team.

Level 2: Mutual Accountability (Individual)

The keys to success in this accountability level include the following seven steps.

1. Initiate communication earlier rather than later. The longer a detrimental behavior lingers on without being addressed, the more difficult the conversation tends to be.

2. Use an informal setting that is comfortable and familiar to the other person, typically his or her classroom.

3. Begin the conversation by establishing common ground and goals for the success of all students.

4. Review the areas of concern that are detrimental to the team. Remember to use factual descriptions of the behaviors in question, and stay away from statements that begin with "I think," "I feel," and "I believe."

5. Tie the areas of concern directly back to the norms and commitments the person has broken. Be sure to focus on the actions instead of the individual, and stay away from statements that begin with "You are" and "You did."

6. Clarify the impact these behaviors have on the team and, ultimately, the students.

7. Work together to establish a plan of action to alter the behaviors in question.

Level 3: Vertical Accountability (Supervisor)

The keys to success in this accountability level include the following six steps.

1. Refrain from involving a supervisor in the previous two levels of accountability.

2. Set a meeting with the supervisor to review the team norms and commitments, the behavior in question, and the steps that you have already taken to correct the issue.

3. Request to be present when the conversation occurs with this person in the event you need to provide clarification.

4. If you are unable to be at the meeting, request a follow-up meeting with the supervisor to receive a summary of the results.

5. When this process concludes, continue the collaborative team process as normal.

6. Should the behavior resurface, keep the supervisor informed with factual statements.

Note that in some cases, the issue separating team members can become personal, and the relationship between members becomes strained and feelings are hurt. How can you rebuild the bridge between team members before the situation turns toxic?

In his book *The Five Disciplines of PLC Leaders*, Timothy D. Kanold (2011) offers several guiding principles to consider when a relationship within the team is becoming volatile. The following are seven effective strategies for approaching this potentially difficult conversation:

1. Confront ASAP: When a relational breakdown occurs between two people on the team, address the issues immediately. Further delay and unresolved issues only complicate the team dynamics.

2. Separate the team member from the wrong action: Most team conflict issues are about a team member's action that undermines the work of the team: for example, failure to be on time, failure to complete an assigned portion of the work

project on time, failure to contribute in a positive manner, failure to act on an agreed-upon project or lesson assessment. It is the team member's actions that need to be addressed, not the quality of the person.

3. Give the team member the benefit of the doubt: It is important not to assume you know why the person was late, failed to deliver the project, or didn't meet the deadline. Allow the person an opportunity to explain his or her actions.

4. Avoid absolute words: Avoid using such words as *always* and *never* ("You *always* let the team down," "You *never* show up on time," "You *never* contribute to our team"). These types of statements are rarely true and diminish the speaker's credibility.

5. Avoid sarcasm: Do not use phrases such as "I know you just think you are too good for us" or "Maybe if you would try just a bit harder you could get it right next time" or "Well, our team knows what you'll be doing while we work on this—nothing!"

6. Tell the team member how you feel about what was done wrong: It is very important to let the team member know how his or her actions made you and/or the team feel. How does the action impact others? Often, offenders to the team norms and values do not fully realize the emotional wake they leave behind because of their actions or inactions in relation to team values and commitments.

7. Keep a short account: Every team encounters some adversity as members debate and argue about important practices and methods for the teaching and learning. Once the *care enough to confront* discussion is completed, everyone on the team must let it go, move on, and keep a short mental account of the issue. Team members who harbor long-term resentments will be toxic to the team's growth. (pp. 108–109)

Conclusion

Be encouraged that people can significantly change their beliefs and behaviors when given the right kind of support. Believing the best of others while following up with reinforcement is the first step to reclaiming disengaged team members. "The final challenge—and the one that solidifies success—is to build so much momentum that change is unstoppable, everything reinforces the new behavior, and even the resistors get onboard, exactly the momentum that develops in winning streaks. That's the virtuous cycle of initiative and performance" (Kanter, 2006, pp. 282–283). Keep in mind, the greatest detractors, when transformed, often make the greatest champions for the cause—so don't give up!

Additional Resources

Teams can use these helpful resources to gain further guidance and insights for their collaborative work.

- *Crucial Conversations: Tools for Talking When Stakes Are High*: Kerry Patterson, Joseph Grenny, Ron McMillan, and Al Switzler (2002) provide a commonsense, practical approach for handling differences of opinion, disagreements, and high-stakes conversations. Drawing from twenty-five years of research on successful communicators, the authors conclude that what sets these people apart from others in their work and personal success is their ability to effectively navigate crucial conversations, regardless of position or power of the people involved.

- *Learning by Doing: A Handbook for Professional Learning Communities at Work* (3rd ed.): In this perennial bestseller, DuFour et al. (2016) address how to deal with conflict in a PLC. In chapter 9, specifically, the authors provide the rationale behind the need to address those in opposition to the new developing culture. They also provide tips for how to approach individuals who continue to resist positive change in the organization.

- *The Five Dysfunctions of a Team*: In this book, Patrick Lencioni (2002) shares a leadership fable about employees in a technology company who are struggling to work together and grow their business. Through the lives of team members in the story, he reveals five foundational building blocks of a team that, when missing, can negatively impact the team and pose potential harm to the organization.

Establishing Clarity on What Students Need to Know and Be Able to Do

Simply put, teacher clarity means an educator has absolute clarity about what students are to learn, know, and be able to do for an upcoming instructional focus before they plan any instruction and assessments.

—Larry Ainsworth

The Story of Ryan Middle School

At Ryan Middle School, the principal makes an effort to spend as much time as possible with collaborative teams to ensure he understands the challenges his teams are facing so he can provide effective and focused support and guidance. During one of these team visits, he realizes that his team members lack clarity regarding learning outcomes and demonstrate inconsistent expectations for students. He finally understands why they do not find value in the data analysis process. The following scenario describes the principal's visit.

The members of the sixth-grade language arts team shuffle into the team leader's classroom ready to learn how their students performed on the common formative assessment (CFA) they gave a few days prior. The team leader kicks off the meeting with a warm welcome, a review of the agenda, and an examination of team norms. This examination focuses on the specific norms team members had developed regarding how they would and would not behave when discussing student evidence. They include the following commitments.

We commit to *do* the following.

- Discuss students as if they and their families were in the room with us, the way we would want teachers to discuss a student who is special to us.

- Celebrate the hard work that our staff engage in each and every day as results are showing up in our data.

- Think critically about what needs to change in *instruction* in order to improve student outcomes.

- Approach areas we are concerned about from a problem-solving outlook.

- Get energized to do more for students through our work with adults.

We will *not* do the following.

- Miss the opportunity to identify and share stories of great growth and increases in proficiency in order to replicate what works well.

- Blame resources or students for a lack of growth or less-than-ideal proficiency. It is our responsibility to deliver high-quality instruction. Instruction changes outcomes for students. Our resources are just that: resources for high-quality instruction. It is how we use the resources that makes the difference for students, but we *do not* attribute limited or high levels of student growth to resources only.

- Get defeated by data.

Following the five-minute norm review, the team leader focuses the team's attention on the Google Doc where teachers entered their class CFA data prior to the meeting. The CFA addresses the following standard: "Determine a theme or central idea of a text and how it is conveyed through particular details; provide a summary of the text distinct from personal opinions or judgments" (RL.6.2; National Governors Association Center for Best Practices [NGA] & Council of Chief State School Officers [CCSSO], 2010). This standard is one of three standards in a four-week unit of instruction focused on theme, textual evidence, plot, and character responses to plot. The teachers do not expect proficiency on the standard until the end of the second trimester, and this CFA takes place during the first trimester, about one week into the unit. It requires students to read a passage, identify the theme, and provide a summary that includes the theme of the passage and the details in the text that convey the theme.

The teachers review the data for the standard and, as expected, the data reveal that most students are not yet demonstrating proficiency. However, two facts are interesting to the team. The first is that students in one teacher's classroom are performing significantly better than the others. Eighty-five percent of the students in this class are already proficient as compared to the other three classrooms, where only 25–30 percent of students are demonstrating proficiency. Second, the team is surprised to see that the nonproficient students struggle with basic understanding of *theme*. As the team discussions continue, it becomes clear to the principal that there is a lack of clarity that might be contributing to the emerging data pattern. He sees this as an opportunity to provide clarity and support to the team and engage in the following discussion.

> **Principal:** What did you discover when unpacking the skills and knowledge embedded in the standard prior to beginning the unit of instruction?
>
> **Teacher A:** We didn't unpack; we didn't have time. We needed to focus on planning the lessons.
>
> **Principal:** Is it possible that each of you prioritized different aspects of the standard or interpreted the expectations of the standard differently?
>
> **Teacher A:** I focused on theme mostly and thought that summary was separate from theme. We spent a lot of time on understanding how to determine a theme and really did not have time to get to summary. I think that is why my students are not yet demonstrating proficiency.
>
> **Teacher B:** I spent a lot of time showing them how to determine theme and then how to connect theme and the details in their summaries. It made sense to me that they should be connected. I think that's why my students did pretty well on the CFA.
>
> **Teacher C:** I wish we had talked about this earlier, because it makes sense. But I also saw these as separate skills.
>
> **Principal:** Who developed the CFA and the rubric?

Teacher A: We divided and conquered. Teacher B developed the CFA, I created the rubric, and Teacher C developed the activities for the unit. Then we came together to review what each of us had done, but we really didn't have a lot of time to spend on it. We had a lot of other things we needed to do. Most of this work was done a few days before the unit started, so we just had to move forward.

When I developed the rubric, I made a section for theme and a section for summary, but maybe I should have created the rubric to show the connections. That would have helped.

Teacher B: We probably should have looked at the CFA together more carefully too. Everything just always seems so rushed, and we don't spend enough time thinking about the outcomes for students. We seem to be focused on teaching more than student learning.

Principal: I agree, it's essential that you gain clarity as a team regarding the standard expectations and outcomes before creating assessments and rubrics and planning for instruction. I suggest you begin planning for the next unit of instruction a few weeks prior to actually beginning instruction. This will give you time as a team, not in isolation as individuals, to gain a deep, collective understanding of the standard; determine the best way to assess it; and define your expectations for proficiency. This clarity ensures that your team examination of student data leads to discussions focused on instructional practices that help students master the standard expectations. Today's discussion provided important insights regarding discrepancies in teacher understanding as opposed to instructional decision making based on accurate data. Let's discuss some ways we can ensure you are prepared for the next unit of instruction.

This discussion leads to specific protocols and practices that the team should engage in to ensure clarity before instruction begins.

High-functioning collaborative teams understand that collective clarity regarding what students should know and be able to do is critical and drives everything they do. They come to consensus about what is crucial for students to learn by determining essential standards for every unit of instruction in every grade and content area or course, and spend time gaining collective understanding of these essential standards and how instruction and assessment should look as a result.

When teams don't have this clarity, they tend to focus on teaching rather than learning, emphasizing instructional activities and resources over collective understanding of the essential outcomes for student learning. Consequently, the instruction, assessment, and data analysis process breaks down; students don't get what they need; and frustration ensues.

This chapter focuses on why this collective clarity is important and provides specific strategies and tools teams can use to achieve it. We'll move on to an overview of what the experts say about what students need to know and be able to do and then continue with how to coach teachers in making sure they understand how to unpack the standards to identify exactly what students need to learn.

What the Experts Say

A guaranteed and viable curriculum is one of the most powerful things a school can implement to help enhance student achievement (DuFour & Marzano, 2011). What does this mean, and how do teams get there? Let's take a closer look. A *guaranteed curriculum* means that all students in a grade level or enrolled in the same course, regardless of the teacher, have an equal opportunity to learn the team's identified essential standards. It is important to emphasize the word *all* in the previous statement. This means that collaborative teams will work hard to ensure that *every* student, no matter what the circumstances, will meet the expectations outlined in each essential standard. They are making a commitment to their students, to themselves, and to the next grade-level teachers that *all* students will receive rigorous instruction, assessment, and intervention aligned to the essential standards.

No longer will what a student learns depend on what teacher a student has. This doesn't mean that teachers must deliver instruction in the same way; instead, the outcomes are the same, but the methods can be different. In fact, this is one way teachers learn from each other when examining student data. They look at student results and begin to examine each other's instructional practices. This is the best job-embedded professional learning there is.

Viable refers to time. Is there a sufficient amount of time available for teachers to teach the content deeply and for students to gain a thorough understanding of it? Typically, the answer is *no*. Teachers describe rushing through content so they can communicate that they covered it. They share frustrations about having too much to teach and concerns that students are missing opportunities to think critically about what they're learning, see connections between topics and ideas, and participate in engaging activities that help them remember content.

Teams can take these two immediate steps to develop a guaranteed and viable curriculum: (1) determine priority standards, sometimes referred to as *essential standards*, *power standards*, or *essential outcomes*; and (2) spend time (at least one week prior to instruction) diving deeply into the unit of instruction to ensure collective clarity about the learning intentions of the priority standards and expectations for mastery. According to Douglas Reeves (2002), "To improve student achievement, educators must determine the power standards—learning standards that are most essential because they possess the qualities of endurance, leverage and readiness for success at the next level" (p. 54). John Hattie (2009) suggests that one of the keys to improving schools is to ensure teachers:

> know the learning intentions and success criteria of their lessons,
> know how well they are attaining these criteria for all their students,
> and know where to go next in light of the gap between students' current knowledge and understanding and the success criteria. (p. 239)

Simply put, this means teams have absolute clarity about what students need to know and be able to do for an upcoming instructional focus *before* they plan instruction and assessments. This clarity ensures that teams are less likely to experience the frustration the team in the opening scenario dealt with due to different interpretations of the standard and expectations for proficiency. When teams are clear before instruction occurs, the data analysis process becomes more meaningful and helps teams determine what to do next to ensure more students learn.

Common Questions About What Students Need to Know and Be Able to Do

Following are the answers to common questions teams might ask regarding prioritizing and unpacking standards and determining proficiency expectations—in other words, identifying what students should know and be able to do.

How Do Teams Develop Priority Standards?

The priority standards process helps teams determine what is absolutely essential for all students to know and be able to do in each grade and content area or course before moving on to the next grade level or course. It does not mean that only the priority standards are important and that teachers won't instruct on others at all; it means that teachers will give priority standards *greater emphasis* in instruction and also assess and offer interventions when students do not demonstrate proficiency.

As Larry Ainsworth (2003) cautions, the process is about prioritization, not elimination. The idea is that the team comes to consensus about the priority standards instead of teachers deciding in isolation what they think is important. The reality is that individual teachers prioritize what they believe is important anyway, so it makes more sense for teams to determine priorities together so students in the same grade or course learn the same things. This leads to a clear and focused plan for common formative assessments and data analysis based on a commitment to ensure *all* students learn the priority standards.

The Simple as 1, 2, 3 Prioritizing Process provides teams with a step-by-step plan for developing priority standards (Friziellie, Schmidt, & Spiller, 2016).

1. Individuals make initial choices based on criteria. Each team member makes an initial assessment of what standards the team should prioritize by studying the three criteria Reeves (2002) outlines: (a) endurance, (b) leverage, and (c) readiness for the next level of learning. The standard must meet one or more of these criteria.

   a. *Endurance* means that the standard reflects learning that will be important now and for a long time to come. For example, in mathematics, a deep understanding of place value is important for students beyond grade school. It isn't something that they will need to know only for a grade level or for a summative assessment.

   b. *Leverage* refers to learning that has cross-curricular implications— something that is taught in one subject but used in another subject. For example, we teach students about unit rate in mathematics but use that concept to solve problems in physical science classes.

   c. *Readiness for the next level of learning* identifies prerequisite skills. For example, in early literacy, students learn letter recognition and sound recognition, which are important skills when learning to read. Students who don't learn letter and sound recognition have a difficult time with future reading skills.

2. After analyzing and discussing these three criteria, each team member reviews the full list of unit standards created in step 1, and takes no more than ten minutes to make his or her initial individual choices regarding what standards to prioritize. Each team member applies professional knowledge and judgment to mark or highlight the standards he or she believes meet one or more of the criteria. This silent thinking time is important to foster individual accountability and avoid groupthink.

Prioritizing step 2 means developing an initial list of priority standards. Teams come to initial conclusions regarding the priority standards list. Teachers share their individual choices using a round-robin structure. One person begins by identifying a standard he or she chose as priority and giving an explanation for his or her choice. Explanations should include how the choice reflects the three criteria of *endurance*, *leverage*, and *readiness for the next level of learning*. What teams do not want to hear is, "I chose this standard because it is something we already do and it will be easy for students to learn."

As each team member shares, others reveal if they also marked that standard and give their explanation and thinking. It is unlikely that there will be full agreement on a particular standard, but if there is, celebrate! If not, the discussion that ensues is often very robust and enlightening. Teachers discover understandings and misunderstandings about the standards that they may not have thought about before. In order for this conversation to be productive and include all voices, determine ahead of time how the team will handle a lack of consensus. The team may decide to develop a list or use a previously developed list of behavioral norms to guide these professional debates. This process continues until all team members are satisfied with their initial list of priority standards.

3. Prioritizing step 3 entails reviewing other sources of information to make final decisions. In this step, team members gather information to help in making a final decision regarding what students need to know and be able to do. A review of the previous and subsequent grade-level, subject-area, and course standards is critical in determining appropriate vertical alignment. For example, in reviewing the subsequent grade-level

standards for mathematics, the team may find that demonstrating a strong understanding of fraction division is necessary for students to be able to master the next learning level. If team members prioritized fraction division, they have taken a positive step toward aligning standards vertically. If not, the team must consider whether to add the standard to its prioritized list.

Whenever possible, teams should consider sharing their initial set of priority standards with the grade levels or courses prior to and after their grade level or course (for example, third grade shares with second grade and fourth grade) to properly ensure strong vertical alignment. Teams can facilitate this process by sharing the list of priority standards electronically and asking team members to provide feedback or by having at least one team member from each grade level or course come together to discuss the vertical progression. If the entire school or district is participating in this process, the vertical alignment component becomes its own step, and teams analyze full priority lists from grade to grade. When engaging in smaller-scale work, this is not always feasible.

Teams will also want to consider information they have from accountability assessments such as state end-of-year tests. This information may include test blueprints, released assessment items, and practice tests, or other documents indicating how much the state assessment emphasizes certain standards. Teams may decide to add other documents to consider, depending on which documents guide teaching and learning in their setting (Bailey, Jakicic, & Spiller, 2014; Reeves, 2002).

How Do Teams Gain Clarity on What Each Essential Standard Means?

Once a team gives curricular priority to standards that are essential for all students to know and be able to do, it needs to engage in the work of gaining shared clarity on what the standards mean and what a proficient student will be able to do. The template in figure 3.1 (page 44) can assist teams in gaining shared clarity on their priority standards.

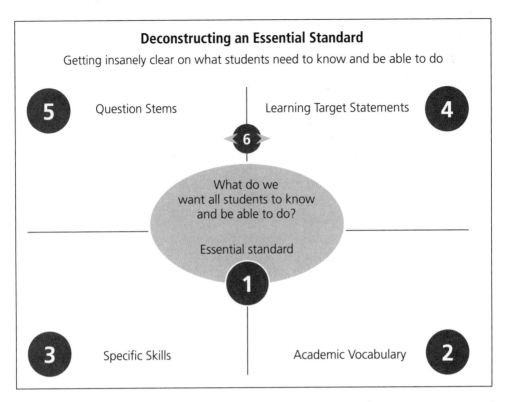

Deconstructing an Essential Standard

Getting insanely clear on what students need to know and be able to do

5 Question Stems
4 Learning Target Statements
6
What do we want all students to know and be able to do?
Essential standard
1
3 Specific Skills
2 Academic Vocabulary

Source: © 2017 by Kris Cunningham. Adapted from Frayer, Frederick, & Klausmeier, 1969. Used with permission.

Figure 3.1: Template for deconstructing an essential standard.

*Visit **go.SolutionTree.com/PLCbooks** for a free reproducible version of this figure.*

Teams should follow these five steps for using the template in figure 3.1.

1. In the center section of the template, the team writes the essential standard in its entirety.

2. The team identifies the academic vocabulary necessary for a student to understand and demonstrate proficiency in the standard. (Front-loading this academic vocabulary prior to instruction in the essential standard is especially helpful for students who traditionally learn at a slower rate.)

3. The team identifies a checklist of specific skills that a student will know and be able to do when proficient in the essential standard.

4. The team examines the essential standard and breaks it into smaller, measurable learning targets. These targets will serve as the basis for a team's common formative assessments. For example, the essential standard states, "Determine a theme or central idea of a text and how it is conveyed through particular details; provide a summary of the

text distinct from personal opinions or judgments" (RL.6.2; NGA & CCSSO, 2010). The standard is much too complex to assess in its entirety, as it requires a student to demonstrate three very distinct skills.

    a. Determine the theme or central idea of a text.

    b. Determine how particular details convey the theme.

    c. Provide a summary of the text distinct from personal opinions or judgments.

As such, following are examples of learning targets for the essential standard.

- The student will be able to define *theme*.

- The student will be able to determine the theme or central idea of a text.

- The student will be able to determine how particular details in the text convey the theme.

- The student will be able to define or describe *summary*.

- The student will be able to provide a summary of the text without personal opinions or judgments.

5. The team determines three to four high-level questions teams could ask students that would provide information about whether the student understands or is proficient in the essential standard.

How Do Teams Ensure Clarity Unit by Unit?

The Pre-Unit Get CLEAR protocol provides teams with an efficient step-by-step process for gaining collective clarity about each unit of instruction before it begins. Teams should participate in this protocol at least one week prior to the beginning of each unit.

The steps of the Pre-Unit Get CLEAR protocol include the following.

- **C:** Create collective understanding.

- **L:** Look at the calendar and devise an instructional plan.

- **E:** Examine assessment administration and attitude.

- **A:** Anticipate student needs and involvement.

- **R:** Review unit rubrics.

Figure 3.2 provides an overview of the Pre-Unit Get CLEAR protocol, including guiding questions to help teams navigate through each step.

Description	Guiding Questions to Consider
Create Collective Understanding	• What is the overall purpose of the unit? • What are the priority standards for this unit? • What is packed inside each standard? (informal unpacking) • Do we all agree on what each learning target looks like instructionally? • What connections are there to other standards or targets? • What would mastery or proficiency look like? • What are the subskills or implicit targets that we must address instructionally for students to demonstrate mastery of each learning target? • Are we clear on how we will use our resources to instruct standards or learning targets? (Review district- or school-approved programs for reading, mathematics, and so on.) • What knowledge and skills do we need as teachers to effectively teach the learning targets? • What will homework look like throughout the unit?
Look at the Calendar and Devise an Instructional Plan	• What CFAs will we devise and issue? • What is our purpose in giving these CFAs? How does each CFA align to our learning goals (skills, learning targets)? • When will during-the-unit CFAs occur? • When will the end-of-unit (summative) CFA occur? • When will we review the data and plan differentiated instructional action steps? • How can we incorporate more unobtrusive assessments?
Examine Assessment Administration and Attitude	• How will we administer the assessment? What logistically do we need to plan? • How will we ensure consistency in test administration? • How can we portray positivity about assessment opportunities and help students feel positive as well? • How do we communicate high expectations for all students no matter what?

Anticipate Student Needs and Involvement	• What does the assessment look like? (Either take the assessment to simulate what students will do or review it carefully as a team.) • Where do we think students will struggle most? • What are the necessary scaffolds for instruction based on individual student needs? • How do we ensure productive struggle versus destructive struggle? • How can we involve students in the assessment process through goal setting, feedback loops, and so on?
Review Unit Rubrics	• What are the mastery or proficiency expectations, as outlined in the rubrics for standards or learning targets assessed during the unit of instruction? • Do we all interpret rubric expectations consistently? • When will collaborative scoring occur to calibrate and check rubric understanding? • How will we communicate suggestions for rubric revisions? • When and how will we share the rubrics with students?

Figure 3.2: Guiding questions for the Pre-Unit Get CLEAR protocol.

*Visit **go.SolutionTree.com/PLCbooks** for a free reproducible version of this figure.*

Create Collective Understanding

In this step, teams think through each of the guiding questions to get clear on the unit purpose, the standards they will teach during the unit, connections to other standards, proficiency expectations, connections to district or school resources, and homework expectations.

Look at the Calendar and Devise an Instructional Plan

The guiding questions direct teams to review the calendar to determine what common formative assessments will be given, when they will administer the assessments, and when they will discuss the data together. Deciding this ahead of time ensures that all team members administer assessments within the same time frame and know exactly when they will discuss data from the assessments as a team.

Examine Assessment Administration and Attitude

In this step, teams discuss how they will administer assessments to students. If each teacher administers assessments differently, the assessment data may not yield reliable results. For example, if one teacher administers the assessment in small groups with a high level of teacher prompting and support and the others administer the assessment to the whole group with limited prompting and support, the team data may indicate that students who took the test in small groups are more proficient when in reality their proficiency was heavily supported by the teacher.

Teacher attitude about the assessment process is a critical factor as well. If teachers communicate positivity about the testing experience and motivate students to do their best, students are more likely to feel good about it. This reminds teachers to be intentionally positive and motivating when discussing all assessments with students. Visit Betsy Weigle's (n.d.) *Classroom Caboodle* blog (https://bit.ly/2JPsZqr) to see a teacher demonstrating a positive mindset about an upcoming unit test for her students.

Anticipate Student Needs and Involvement

In this step, teams actually take the assessment that they will be giving to students so they can experience what their students will experience. They do this to ensure that the test measures what they intend it to measure and identify any confusing questions that could affect the reliability of the results. In addition, teams should identify where they think students will struggle and how they can adjust instruction to ensure students understand the concepts clearly. They consider what instructional scaffolds are necessary for the different types of learners in their classrooms while remembering to keep expectations high for all students. Teams will also consider how to involve students in the assessment process so they become more invested as learners.

Review Unit Rubrics

Finally, teams review the proficiency expectations outlined in the rubrics and adjust them based on what they discovered while reviewing the assessment during step 4. This step provides an opportunity for teams to consider how each team member interprets the rubric expectations and decide when they will score collaboratively to calibrate and check rubric understanding. It is not always feasible for a full collaborative scoring process to occur, but when teams engage frequently in this discussion, it's more likely that rubric interpretation will be consistent. Teams should share rubrics with students as a way of defining their expectations. Teams should discuss and determine a plan for how students will experience and understand the rubrics prior to assessment.

The five steps of the Pre-Unit Get CLEAR protocol may seem overwhelming, and the first time through the process may take a significant amount of time.

However, the protocol will begin to go faster once teams are familiar with the steps and have more structures in place aligned to the expectations. For example, if a team does not have clear priority standards, then it may take more time before it can engage in collective understanding about each standard (as outlined in step 1 of the protocol). Once team members determine priority standards for each unit, they can review each standard so they can align instruction accordingly.

When teams are intentional about gaining this collective clarity before a unit begins, the entire teaching, assessing, and intervention process is more purposeful and meaningful. Data will provide reliable information that teachers can respond to so all students are learning at high levels.

How to Coach Your Team

Teams need support as they go through the process of gaining clarity. If there are team leaders for grade-level teams or department heads for content-alike teams in your system, build the capacity of these team members to lead and facilitate this work. Leaders should understand why this work is important and know how to help their teams when they have questions about the process. When team members feel like they don't understand why the work is important or they are unclear about how to approach the work, they often participate in the process out of compliance. They do it because they were told to, not because they value the work or find it meaningful. Knowledgeable team leaders or department heads can be extremely helpful in guiding teams and reminding them why the work is important. However, if you don't have team leaders or department heads in your school, teams can identify someone who will learn more about the process and facilitate the team. This can be a rotating role for different aspects of the work teams engage in.

Principals or assistant principals can play a vital role in coaching teams by engaging in five critical actions.

1. They communicate the expectation that teams create a guaranteed and viable curriculum at their school, and that teams have a clear answer to PLC critical question 1: What do students need to know and be able to do?

2. They support teams in meeting these expectations by providing necessary professional learning so teams understand why it is important and how to do the work.

3. They provide time for teams to participate in the work.

4. They provide guidance and support for teams to be successful and find value in the work.

5. They monitor what they expect and hold teams accountable for the work.

In the scenario at the beginning of this chapter, the principal asks the team, "What did you discover when unpacking the skills and knowledge embedded in the standard prior to beginning the unit of instruction?" The way he asks the question includes a positive presupposition that the team has already unpacked the standard prior to beginning the unit. Teacher A responds that the team has not unpacked the standard because it did not have time. However, the principal frames the question in a way that communicates the importance he places on this expectation. Through continued questioning, team members come to the conclusion that they need to take the time to have these critical conversations before diving into a unit of instruction. The principal does not have to tell them what they should do; he coaches them by asking important questions. When there is a lack of engagement or expectation from leadership, team members can do this by asking similar questions of each other as they engage in the work.

Conclusion

The protocols and processes in this chapter provide tools for collaborative teams to keep the focus on learning and ensure that all team members are on the same page. Students will benefit from the collective wisdom gained when teams take the time to unravel the complexities of learning and assessment prior to engaging in instruction.

Additional Resources

Teams can use these helpful resources to gain further guidance and insights for their collaborative work.

- **Power Standards: Identifying the Standards That Matter the Most**: In this 2003 publication, Larry Ainsworth walks readers through the rationale and steps for developing power standards. This resource also provides information about how to use power standards in teaching and learning to significantly improve student achievement.

- ***Prioritizing the Common Core: Identifying Specific Standards to Emphasize the Most:*** Larry Ainsworth (2013) offers an updated version of *Power Standards: Identifying the Standards That Matter the Most* with this text that renames the process to priority standards in order to clearly articulate that the process does not expect elimination of standards, only prioritization of those deemed by the team as most important. Another difference from the original *Power Standards* text is the focus on how to specifically prioritize the more rigorous Common Core standards; standards based on the Common Core; or other next-generation, more complex standards. It includes a step-by-step process for determining what is most important in the Common Core.

- ***Common Formative Assessment: A Toolkit for Professional Learning Communities at Work:*** In this book, Kim Bailey and Chris Jakicic (2011) address the importance of formative assessment in ensuring *all* students learn at high levels. They offer suggestions, tools, and protocols for teams to make this work more effective, manageable, and productive. They address the importance of rubrics and many other ideas included in the Pre-Unit Get CLEAR protocol.

- ***Collaborating for Success With the Common Core: A Toolkit for Professional Learning Communities at Work:*** This 2014 book by Bailey et al. addresses the critical work teams must engage in as part of a PLC focused on ensuring all students learn the Common Core standards or any more rigorous, next-generation state standards. This book outlines a procedure for identifying essential standards, helps teams grapple with determining proficiency expectations, and outlines a process for developing high-quality assessments.

Planning for Targeted and Effective Team Interventions

Many of life's failures are men who did not realize how close they were to success when they gave up.

—Thomas Edison

The Story of Spivey Elementary School

Mrs. Cathy is a third-grade teacher at Spivey Elementary School (SES). As she staples the new border to her bulletin board, she cannot help but wonder if this will finally be the year SES makes huge gains in student achievement. Mrs. Cathy began her education career four years ago as a third-grade mathematics teacher. While she and her team have had ups and downs, they have made great strides in becoming a high-functioning collaborative team.

SES began its journey to become a PLC several years before. Teams routinely work together to clarify what students will learn in each grade level and content area, and have even determined what mastery-level work looks like for each skill. Teams have developed common formative assessments that they frequently administer to assess student mastery of each learning standard. In fact, teacher teams have become experts in using information gathered from those assessments to improve their practices as educators.

However, the teachers at Spivey Elementary are very protective of their students. They believe that because they have built such strong

relationships with their students, they are the only people uniquely qualified to help struggling students in their classes. Because of this belief, they
don't feel the need to share student-specific data with one another or plan
for interventions together. With this prevailing view of student assistance,
each teacher is responsible for identifying his or her students who need
additional help, assigning them to specific tutorial times, and coming up
with suitable reteaching methods.

Some students have grown due to the teams' efforts, but unfortunately,
many students have not made the progress SES was expecting when it
began implementing the PLC process. To increase achievement, administration commits to reassigning two teachers to act as instructional support for students in mathematics and reading for the coming year. They
will primarily pull out small groups of students who show a deficiency in
one or more skills in an attempt to close the learning gap. While teachers
are thankful for this additional support, they are collectively concerned
that it may not be enough given the number of students who have learning difficulties throughout the year.

Unfortunately, the story of Spivey Elementary is all too familiar for many
well-meaning schools. In some of these schools, the desire to ensure learning for
all students is alive and well, and the initial building blocks of a high-functioning
PLC are in place. Learning is the fundamental purpose of the school, and the collaborative culture is focused primarily on how well the system ensures learning for
every student. Collaborative teams are answering the first two critical questions in
a PLC (DuFour et al., 2016).

1. What do students need to know and be able to do?

2. How will we know if they learned it?

While coming to consensus on the answers to the first two critical questions is
certainly beneficial to the learning process, answering those questions alone will
not overcome the significant learning gaps that some students face on a daily basis.

We have watched teacher after teacher spend hours researching, planning, organizing materials, and setting up their rooms with precision in an effort to deliver
the most effective lessons possible. The ultimate hope is for those dynamic lessons
to meet the learning needs of each student. Yet, we find that almost every learning
experience produces three types of learners in the classroom: (1) students who
already understood the concept prior to the lesson, (2) students who learn the
concept during the lesson, and (3) students who do not learn the concept during

the lesson. Since not all students learn in the same way or at the same rate, the collaborative teams in a PLC account for these differences by planning for them ahead of time. In addition to gaining clarity on what students should learn and how they will assess student learning, teams address the final two critical questions for learning (DuFour et al., 2016).

3. How will we respond if they don't learn it?

4. How will we extend the learning for those who know it?

In this chapter, we will address common pitfalls that cause teams to stumble when planning for additional time and support for student learning. In doing so, we will provide strategies for how to avoid and overcome those missteps to ensure each student receives the support he or she needs.

What the Experts Say

An effective intervention system begins with the classroom teacher delivering solid core instruction. In a PLC, the teacher works collaboratively with other team members who share a common learning goal to determine what strategies have proven to be most effective for student learning. This practice is a powerful tool. Robert J. Marzano (2010) says this about identifying best practices:

> Educational research is not a blunt instrument that shatters all doubt about best practice. Rather it provides general direction that must be interpreted by individual districts, schools, and teachers in terms of their unique circumstances. In short, research will never be able to identify instructional strategies that work with every student in every class. The best research can do is tell us which strategies have a good chance (i.e., high probability) of working well with students. Individual classroom teachers must determine which strategies to employ with the right students at the right time. In effect, a good part of effective teaching is an art. (p. 5)

Considering that thought, the first priority for any teacher looking to improve student learning is always to draw from the expertise of other educators on the team. No one else knows your students or what specific strategies are working as well as the team does. This regular practice of self-reflecting and analyzing effective classroom practices is an excellent way to improve core classroom instruction. Keep in mind, an outstanding system of interventions will never overcome poor class-room instruction. But what do we do when some students do not learn the essential standards despite receiving solid core instruction?

When students struggle in school, the research and evidence in our field have never been more conclusive about the solution—RTI is the right way to intervene. In fact, researcher John Hattie's (2009) meta-analysis of more than eighty thousand studies comparing the factors that impact student learning concludes that RTI ranks in the top-three practices proven to most significantly increase student achievement (Buffum et al., 2018). The average yearly impact rate of a well-implemented system of RTI has a standard deviation of 1.29 (Killian, 2017). By comparison, a 1.0 standard deviation increase is typically associated with advancing student achievement by two to three years in just one year's time (Hattie, 2009).

A response to intervention system is traditionally organized into a pyramid to indicate various types of support, who is responsible for implementing that support, and how a student qualifies to move in and out of supports. For example, figure 4.1 identifies three different tiers, or levels, of support for students. Each level is unique in what it provides for students. When used with fidelity at every level, a system modeled after this system of supports ensures each student receives the help he or she needs to improve learning.

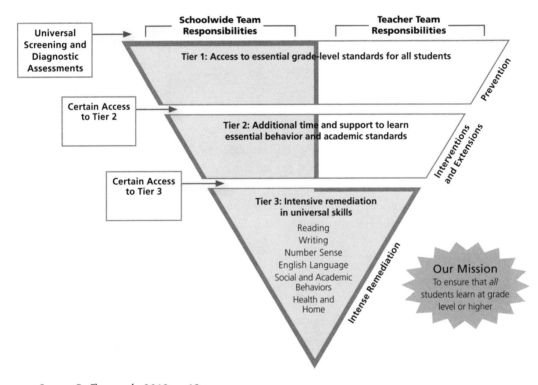

Source: Buffum et al., 2018, p. 18.

Figure 4.1: The RTI at Work pyramid.

The goal of any system of intervention is to close the gap between what students know and what teachers want them to know. The challenge, however, is that to close the learning gap, students must make more than one year's growth in learning in just one year. That idea alone presents challenges for educators. The amount of content a student is required to learn (by state or national standards) each year greatly surpasses the amount of time available; yet a student who has fallen behind in understanding content must learn at a faster rate than his or her peers. While this may seem counterintuitive, it is the exact issue RTI was designed to address.

Common Questions About Targeted and Effective Team Interventions

Even though effective RTI implementation is the best way to address common challenges that teams face, well-intentioned teams often struggle when attempting to provide students with more targeted and effective time. Reasons for this include the following.

- Teachers rely on average scores rather than gathering information by student, by standard.

- The number of students who need additional support is more than the system is designed to handle.

- There is a lack of expertise or training in how to intervene for a particular deficit.

- The type of support provided is the same for all students, regardless of the cause of the deficiency.

- There are limited resources, including time, space, and staff available to provide support.

The ability to erase the achievement gap for a student begins with a team's capacity to overcome these challenges. Teams can readily address and improve the first four challenges. However, the last challenge requires resources or supports that are often found outside the team itself. In the last part of this chapter, we will discuss practical ways to mitigate these common stumbling blocks.

Following are the answers to common questions teams might ask regarding providing effective and targeted interventions for students at all levels of learning.

What Data Should Teams Use to Determine Appropriate Interventions?

A critical part of the teaching and learning cycle for a team is collecting and analyzing data regarding student learning. Some teams suffer from DRIP (data rich, information poor) syndrome. These teams collect mountains of data from a particular assessment, only to become lost in the vast amount of information available. To be effective, teams must narrow down the scope of the data to the needs of each student.

Other teams are excellent at determining what is essential to learn and creating common ways to assess student learning; yet they stop short of gathering relevant information regarding each student's learning. Often, teams use overall averages on a skill or assessment to determine the type or intensity of the support they give. For example, after giving a common assessment, Mrs. Cathy might find that twelve of her twenty-five students did not pass the test. Because they did not meet the minimum expectation, she is considering bringing them in during recess so she can go over the questions they missed and provide tutorials. While this is a good-faith effort on her part, we would urge Mrs. Cathy to become more targeted with the assistance she provides. Instead of using overall averages, a better method is to break down the information by student, by standard. By analyzing data in this way, we are able to give the right students the right help while limiting the time and resources spent on students who may otherwise not need additional assistance. Figure 4.2 shows a simple way to organize data to ensure all students receive the specific help they need.

How Do Teams Ensure All Students Get the Support They Need?

In 1889, the South Fork Dam broke and sent over twenty million gallons of water from Lake Conemaugh cascading toward the town of Johnstown, Pennsylvania. Locals were warned ahead of time that the dam's structure was compromised and the pressure might cause it to give way. Sadly, people in the area mostly ignored these warnings. To this day, it is still the deadliest dam collapse in U.S. history, with the lost lives numbering more than two thousand.

Unfortunately, traditional systems of support for students fall under much the same demise as the South Fork Dam. The structure is made weaker by a variety of factors, the most prevalent being too many students who need support compared to the number of staff available to help them. When that happens, the system gives

Team:	Date:		Essential Standards Assessed:	
Student Name	Mastered Skill or Skills	Extension or Enrichment	Deficient Skill or Skills	Intervention
1.				
2.				
3.				
4.				
5.				
6.				
7.				
8.				
9.				
10.				
11.				
12.				
13.				
14.				
15.				
16.				
17.				
18.				
19.				
20.				

Figure 4.2: Student data tracking by student name and need.

*Visit **go.SolutionTree.com/PLCbooks** for a free reproducible version of this figure.*

way, and instead of water gushing through the dam, frustration and discouragement surge through the faculty. Despite their hard work and desire to see all students excel, the system of support lies in ruin, and student learning is the casualty.

Just as the people of Johnstown had signs of the dangers ahead, we, too, have red flags warning of potential disaster with our systems of support. We have heard the pleas of countless teachers who are attempting to implement improvement measures but are overwhelmed by the sheer number of students who need intervention or remediation. Thankfully, teachers have a fail-safe way to improve this dilemma that is simple and effective: resist the urge to intervene on every skill. Instead of assessing and intervening on every possible skill to which a student may be exposed, focus your attention, efforts, and resources only on skills the team identifies as essential for students to learn. Aligning the practice of identifying only students who need additional time or support in learning the essentials will help reduce the overall number of students in the system.

What Are the Best Resources for Effective Interventions?

Not only should we ensure the correct students receive help in the right areas, but we should also ensure they receive the right remedy. Each teacher has unique strengths and areas in which he or she excels. This fact reveals itself when teams routinely compare common formative assessment results with one another. When teams find activities, processes, or resources that produce better results than others, they should apply those best practices to students who need additional support. If no team member produces strong results in an area of need, the team should seek out additional professional development for that skill. Figure 4.3 shows a chart that the teams at Brownsboro High School in Brownsboro, Texas, use to help guide the conversation about best practices in the classroom.

How Do Teams Help Students Who Are Still Falling Behind?

In late April 2009, Brandon's father, Robert Jones, developed a sore throat. After taking over-the-counter medication for a couple of weeks with no relief, he decided it was time to see his general physician. His doctor prescribed an antibiotic for what he diagnosed as a sinus infection. Despite two rounds of medication, the sore throat did not get any better. The doctor then gave Robert steroids for what he concluded must be a viral infection. This, too, provided no relief. Unfortunately, it wasn't until months later that a surgeon took a biopsy of Robert's throat to determine the actual

Name		Date	
Team Name		Assessment Date	

Essential Standards				
Standard	Highest Percentage Mastered (From Any Team Member)	Percentage of My Students Mastered	What Caused the Best Results? (Use to Enrich and Intervene)	What Did Not Work? (Remove This Practice)

Questions in Need of Review		
Question Number	Concern	Proposed Change

Scope and Sequence		
Standard or Topic	Concern	Proposed Change

Source: © 2019 by Brownsboro High School. Used with permission.

Figure 4.3: Programmatic data analysis.

*Visit **go.SolutionTree.com/PLCbooks** for a free reproducible version of this figure.*

cause of the pain—stage 4 cancer. Almost a decade after surgery, chemotherapy, and radiation treatments, Robert is a walking miracle and still cancer-free! And while this story has a happy ending, we cannot help but wonder what would have happened if no one decided to look for the *root cause* of the sore throat.

Unfortunately, teams are sometimes guilty of the same type of thinking. Instead of asking critical questions about the root cause for a student's lack of learning, they rely on overall averages, final grade reports, and standardized test scores to determine the type of additional support a student will receive. In the book *Taking Action*, Buffum et al. (2018) describe two primary causes for students' struggling in school. Some students lack the *skills* necessary to master specific academic essentials, while others lack the *will* to master the essentials. Students with *skill* needs require support with a specific academic skill, while students with *will* needs require support with an essential academic behavior (Buffum et al., 2018). Table 4.1 shows a few examples of how each type of need might manifest itself in the classroom.

Table 4.1: Skill and Will Needs

Skill Needs	Will Needs
The universal screener reveals the student is missing prerequisite skills.	The student refuses to complete homework assignments.
A formative assessment reveals the student did not master one or more essential standards.	The student disengages during direct teaching time, which leads to frustration during classwork.
Academic vocabulary is preventing the student from mastering the concept of the day.	The student acts out during class in an effort to detract from the learning of the day.
The student routinely asks clarifying questions during instruction in an effort to understand but continues to make simple mistakes during independent practice.	The student distracts other members of the group during a collaborative task in an attempt to get out of doing the work.

Identifying which of these primary causes is at the root of a student's not learning the essentials is a critical step in providing the right type of intervention. As you can see from the examples in table 4.1, students with a skill need typically give full effort during the learning process but continue to struggle in learning the desired concepts. In contrast, students with a will need typically act in a way that distracts or detracts from the learning in an effort to avoid the work.

The most common mistake in this part of the process is putting all students in the same type of intervention, regardless of the cause. That would be the equivalent of giving all patients with a sore throat the same medication, regardless of the actual cause. Separating students who need these different types of support allows teams to provide academic skill intervention to those who need it while making sure that others who need academic behavioral intervention receive that.

Figure 4.4 (page 64) is an organizational chart from *Uniting Academic and Behavior Interventions* (Buffum, Mattos, Weber, & Hierck, 2015) that individuals or teams may use to help link targeted outcomes with interventions specific to the root cause of the lack of learning.

Figure 4.5 (page 65) offers a protocol with guiding questions to help drive the conversation about skill versus will interventions for students. We originally developed this for an intervention team, but the questions are also applicable for teacher teams.

What Support Should Teams Expect From Campus Administrators?

In a perfect world, each district and campus would have the resources and staff to ensure each student receives one-on-one instruction with a highly qualified instructor. Since no schools operate in that world, we must critically analyze and maximize the use of each resource available to ensure learning for all. Administrators serve a key role in this process because they oversee financial and physical resources as well as allocation of time, that most precious resource to teacher teams. As teams work to gather correct information, identify the correct students, and ensure the correct practices are in place for intervention, campus- and district-level leadership must begin by taking a critical look at all logistical components of the process. Leaders should consider the following four items when supporting teams.

1. **Time (teachers):** Teachers need protected time set aside within the normal (contractual) school day to review student data and plan for interventions. The amount of time necessary may vary from team to team. Administrators and leaders must keep this time sacred for the teachers and not allow other events to interrupt, such as parent-teacher conferences, individualized education plan (IEP) meetings, and staff meetings. Time built into the contractual school day to collaborate is essential to the PLC collaborative team process. There are many ways that schools can accomplish this. For example:

   ○ Common grade-level or common course preps

   ○ Specified time once a week that teams meet

   ○ Specified time during the week when the whole school meets

   ○ Professional development days specified for team collaboration

Student: _____   **Meeting Date:** _____

Participants: _____

	Targeted Outcomes	Concern	Cause	Desired Outcomes	Intervention Steps	Who Takes Responsibility
Led by Teacher Teams	Grade-level essential standards					
	Immediate prerequisite skills					
	English language					
Led by Schoolwide Teams	Academic behaviors					
	Social behaviors					
	Health and home					

Next Meeting Date: _____

Source: Buffum et al., 2015.

Figure 4.4: Intervention targeting process.

*Visit **go.SolutionTree.com/PLCbooks** for a free reproducible version of this figure.*

As intervention teams meet each week to discuss students' academic and behavior supports, answer the following questions as you identify the cause and provide targeted time and support.

1. **Symptom:** In three sentences or less, what specifically is happening with the student?

2. **Cause:** What is the root cause?

3. **Target:** In reviewing our school's system of interventions, what is the targeted intervention we will use to support this student?

4. **Monitor:** Who will be responsible for monitoring the impact of the intervention?

5. **Communication:** What specific information do we need to share with teachers that will help?

6. **Re-evaluation:** Did the intervention work after one to two weeks? If not, what is the next targeted intervention we will use to support this student?

Figure 4.5: Guiding questions for team intervention.

*Visit **go.SolutionTree.com/PLCbooks** for a free reproducible version of this figure.*

- o Assemblies and other scheduled events

- o Rotation of substitutes into the rooms of teachers who need time

2. **Space:** Teachers may need additional space to provide targeted interventions. Be creative with common areas, small meeting rooms, and office areas to accommodate teachers who may need to work with smaller or larger groups of students. When additional learning for students is the priority, no room is off limits for use.

3. **Time (students):** By far, the number-one reason administrators and leaders give for not being able to provide students with additional time and support for learning is that the master schedule will not allow for it. This argument is simply unjustifiable since administration, in large part, controls the design of the master schedule. Schools routinely create alternate schedules for early release days, guest speakers, fire drills, and pep assemblies. Why, then, is it so difficult to create an alternate schedule for students to receive additional support in learning? We urge administrators to take a critical look at the time allocated for intervention and alter the master schedule as necessary.

4. **Framework:** Another support administrators may provide is a big-picture framework of how and when teams will review data and implement interventions. This information provides guideposts for teams to follow to ensure they are providing interventions in a timely manner. Figure 4.6 (page 66) is a sample framework of the intervention process for teams.

Time	Monitor	Tools or Evidence	Completed
First Week of School Tier 3	Teams should place students in Tier 3 intensive interventions based on a universal screening process. Ideally, teams should provide universal screening for reading, writing, numeracy, English language, behavior, and attendance.	Quick write Standardized Test for the Assessment of Reading (STAR) Reading passage or summary Self-Administered Gerocognitive Exam (SAGE) data Dynamic Indicators of Basic Early Literacy Skills (DIBELS) data Reading or writing screeners	
Second Week of School Norms	Each collaborative team establishes norms, norm check procedures, and a plan to review and revise norms throughout the year (for example, at the end of each quarter).	Team norms	
Third Week of School Guaranteed and Viable Curriculum	Each collaborative team answers the question, "What will students learn during this unit, quarter, trimester, or semester (essential standards)?" It is critical that this list be relatively focused, because the following actions apply only to those standards teams have prioritized for all students to master in a course. Teams should communicate essential standards to students in student-friendly language.	Essential standards Endurance, readiness, and leverage Learning target worksheet	
Fourth Week of School Common Formative Assessment	Each team develops and uses at least one common formative assessment (CFA) directly linked to the essential standards or learning targets. • The CFA should measure student achievement at the learning target level. (This means the team must unwrap essential standards into measurable targets.) • Teams use CFAs to provide students with mid-unit interventions that precede summative assessments. • Teams also use CFAs to compare results teacher to teacher. Teachers should provide examples of how these comparisons have actually impacted their own and their teams' instruction.	Data sheet	

Time	Monitor	Tools or Evidence	Completed
Fifth Week of School **Interventions**	Each team develops a way to provide additional time and support to students who struggle with the essential standards identified by the fourth week of school. • Teams use information gathered from CFAs at the learning target level. • Teams provide this support prior to any summative assessment on these essential standards. Teams provide support based on a collective strategy or schedule, rather than each teacher providing sole support to his or her own students. This exemplifies the thinking, "How do we best support our students?" • Teams should monitor progress at least every two weeks in order to determine how students are responding to this additional support. • Teams should place students who are not responding sufficiently to interventions in Tier 3 intensive interventions, as discussed by the school's intervention team.	Intervention plan	
Sixth Week of School **Extensions**	Each team develops a way to provide extensions to students who demonstrate that they have already learned the essential standards. • Extensions are based on information from CFAs at the target level. • Teams provide extensions prior to any summative assessment on the essential standards. • Extensions are not busywork or more work. They represent a deeper application of learning or require students to demonstrate their understanding in another way (for example, a project).	Extension activities during flex time	

Figure 4.6: Sample district pacing process.

continued →

Time	Monitor	Tools or Evidence	Completed
Seventh Week of School **Evidence**	School administrators begin meeting with teams to do the following. • Examine evidence that teams provide. • Discuss obstacles that teams face. • Understand how to support the teams. (Note: If at all possible and time permits, all school administrators [principal and assistant principals] should meet with each team. If not, it is essential that the principal be involved in the process and not delegate the entire process to assistant principals.)	Five monitoring questions	
Eighth Week of School **Evidence**	District administrators begin meeting with school leadership teams to do the following. • Examine evidence that the school produces. • Discuss obstacles that the school faces. • Understand how to support the school. • Understand districtwide trends and needs. • Discuss use of the information to improve.	PLC site visit form	

Repeat this process each quarter.

Source: Adapted from © 2016 by Austin Buffum. Used with permission.

Visit go.SolutionTree.com/PLCbooks for a free reproducible version of this figure.

How to Coach Your Team

The need for a highly effective team is never more evident than when trying to meet the wide range of student needs. Doing so requires a collaborative effort on the part of every team member that begins long before delivering the intervention. To gauge your team's or school's preparedness to help every student succeed, use the guide in figure 4.7 (page 70).

When completing this guide as a team, pay close attention to the areas that fall in the Full Implementation column. These may be areas of growth or improvement for your team. Being intentional and making incremental steps forward to full implementation in all areas will increase your team's ability to provide the additional time and support each student needs to be successful.

In addition, take time to recognize the areas that are already in place and well established. You should not let the efforts of your team go unnoticed; any movement toward helping students is a cause for celebration. Though the task will seem daunting at times, press forward and know that your venture to provide all students the specific support they need will make an instrumental difference in their learning experience.

Conclusion

Meeting individual learning needs can be a daunting task for any one person to undertake. It takes the unrelenting efforts of all members of the collaborative team to make it work. Without a doubt, intervening for each student "by name, by need" is one of the tempting stopping places on the journey to become an effective PLC. By focusing your efforts on a limited number of critical skills, identifying the root cause of the student's lack of learning, and allocating resources in a meaningful way, your team will be well on your way to ensuring high levels of learning for all students! With that, our team echoes our mentor, Richard DuFour (2002), as we urge you to have the passion and persistence to "press on!"

Indicator of Preparedness	Degree of Preparedness				
	Full Implementation	Partial Implementation	Limited Implementation	Not in Place	Don't Know
All educators understand that RTI is a buildingwide framework designed to benefit all students, not solely students in special education.					
The school allocates sufficient time and resources to teams, teachers, and professional development in support of the RTI components.					
All educators within a team have collaboratively agreed on a limited number of essential standards for all students to learn.					
Ongoing work to align the essential standards with state or national standards is evident.					
All educators participate in developing and administering frequent common formative assessments.					
Teams have a means or a tool by which to gather information from common formative assessments by student, by standard.					
Teams use information gathered from common formative assessments to determine the specific academic needs of each student.					
All educators understand the roles and responsibilities they play, as well as those of their colleagues, to maximize capacity for student support.					

Degree of Preparedness					
Indicator of Preparedness	Full Implementation	Partial Implementation	Limited Implementation	Not in Place	Don't Know
All educators use information gathered from common formative assessments to determine best practices of instruction for each skill. They use these best practices to intervene for students deficient in each skill.					
All educators understand the importance of sharing students within the team to ensure all students receive the additional support they need.					
Teams provide students with a variety of supplemental interventions based on the root cause of their needs (for example, failed learner versus intentional nonlearner).					
All educators take into consideration the reason for a student's deficiency in learning and assign students to supplemental support accordingly.					
The school schedule allows for maximum use of resources in the core classes and for daily, tiered supplemental intervention time.					

Source: Adapted from Windram, Bollman, & Johnson, 2012.

Figure 4.7: Team preparedness for meeting diverse student needs.

Visit go.SolutionTree.com/PLCbooks for a free reproducible version of this figure.

Additional Resources

Teams can use these helpful resources to gain further guidance and insights for their collaborative work.

- *Taking Action: A Handbook for RTI at Work*: In this book, Buffum et al. (2018) provide a comprehensive guide for RTI and getting the right students the right help. This in-depth study introduces the history and purpose of RTI and also dispels common misunderstandings. Building on previous works, which include *Pyramid Response to Intervention* (Buffum et al., 2009) and *Simplifying Response to Intervention* (Buffum, Mattos, & Weber, 2012), this book is the most complete compilation of RTI explanations and resources available.

- *Uniting Academic and Behavior Interventions: Solving the Skill or Will Dilemma*: In this book, Austin Buffum et al. (2015) take the reader through a step-by-step process for determining, targeting, and observing academic and behavior interventions that ensure students' long-term success.

- *Learning by Doing: A Handbook for Professional Learning Communities at Work* (**3rd ed.**): In this perennial bestseller, DuFour et al. (2016) answer the questions of *why* and *how* about responding when students don't learn. In chapter 7, specifically, the authors provide tips for how to create systematic interventions to ensure students receive additional time and support for learning.

Working Together in a PLC

Clarity precedes competence.

—Mike Schmoker

The Story of Caribou Elementary School

Caribou Elementary School is a kindergarten through fifth-grade school that has relied on the social capital provided by its suburban setting. There are few academic or behavioral concerns, and its standardized test scores are consistently well above the state average. The neighborhood has supportive families, zero attendance issues, and few situations of poverty.

District leaders and administration fully embrace the PLC process and have provided support by establishing the expectation that teams will meet weekly during the allocated time at the building level. Although the school has progressed in their PLC journey, teams throughout the building are functioning at very different stages along the PLC continuum, and some teams are far from realizing the shared mission of ensuring learning for all. The first- and third-grade teachers, in particular, continue to struggle with clarity, feeling a need to function independently and teach the way they always have.

The first-grade teachers take their lessons directly from a scripted basal series, other purchased programs, or previous lessons from previous years. Repeatedly, the administration has reminded them to follow the four critical questions of a PLC (DuFour et al., 2016) and begin determining what is essential for students to know and be able to do. However, these teachers continually push back and take the stance that what they've done has worked for many years and has been effective for most students.

Ms. Martinez, the first-grade team leader, has done her research and tends to agree with the administration that simply covering content isn't ensuring high levels of learning for all.

After having numerous discussions with her colleagues and trying to convince them that their plans and materials from a decade ago are designed for different students with different needs, she has become frustrated and unable to move this group of individuals to become a team focused on student learning.

While the teachers collectively appreciate the concept of identifying what is essential and the idea that they will be able to focus on less material to cover, individually they are committed to ensuring they cover and follow the district-provided materials. As one grade-level team member states, "Doing it this way throughout my career, I've done what the district has told us to do, and I've covered my backside." Another teacher fears he will lose individual autonomy and creativity within the classroom to do what he believes is best, stating, "We were hired to teach first grade."

Meanwhile, the third-grade team is extremely compliant and rarely strays from school direction, yet team members aren't fully committed to the four critical questions. They get along beautifully, and nobody ever questions their dedication to the job because they work tirelessly, well beyond contractual hours, to individually meet the needs of the twenty-five students within the four walls of their respective classrooms. Yet they continue to struggle to meet the needs of all students across the grade level. This team continually wonders why its scores aren't higher on the end-of-year assessment because team members feel they have done what the administration has asked them to do.

Mrs. Smith, the third-grade team leader, has taken on the responsibility of creating the team's weekly agenda and putting it on the action plan. The team members have gone through many of the steps, such as establishing team norms and creating a SMART goal, yet rarely revisit them until the principal reminds them to do so. SMART goals must be specific, measurable, attainable, results oriented, and time bound (O'Neill & Conzemius, 2013).The header of the agenda is even stamped with the four critical questions in bold, followed by a prioritized list of topics, the first of which covers upcoming grade-level and school events, immediately followed by lunchroom, playground, and restroom issues.

Unfortunately, the third-grade team meeting rarely gets off the ground, and one team member, Mr. Jones, typically hijacks the meeting by sharing his disgruntled opinions around student behavior and lack of administrative support. While the other three team members are interested in addressing the remaining items on the agenda, such as what needs to happen with the essential standards they have begun to identify and their plan for assessment, the topics of student behavior and poor administrative support end up monopolizing the discussion.

The first-grade and third-grade teams are making some strides to becoming a highly functioning PLC, yet they continue to struggle to achieve competence because they have not gained clarity to move forward. Team members need to begin working interdependently and using the four critical questions as the moral compass that directs their work.

When teacher teams have a clear understanding of what administration and their colleagues expect from them, when they become aligned to the four critical questions of a PLC, when they assume collective responsibility for the learning of all students across their team and school, and when they maintain a mission of ensuring learning for all students, they will begin moving toward a true PLC. This chapter provides tools and strategies for your team to find clarity and begin to push through these common challenges to achieve competence.

What the Experts Say

While the previous scenario has an elementary frame, the scenario plays out across all levels, all schools, and all demographics, worldwide. As Schmoker (2004) states in the epigraph of this chapter, "Clarity precedes competence" (p. 85), and many educators attempt to hold on to methods and systems that are proven *not* to work because there is no clarity around the expectations. When we function as a PLC, we interdependently become very clear and highly competent on a few key components in order to effectively ensure high levels of learning for all students. This foundation is unified through four pillars that provide clarity to produce professional competence in ensuring high levels of student learning.

1. **Shared purpose:** What is our mission?

2. **Shared vision:** What is our compelling future?

3. **Collective commitments:** How will we behave to reach our vision?

4. **Shared goals:** What are our targets and time lines?

Figure 5.1 shows the PLC structure in the form of a building with four pillars resting securely on a strong foundation.

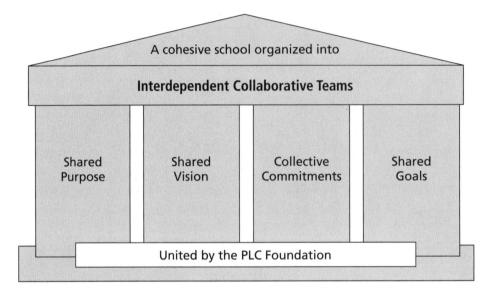

Source: Adapted from DuFour, DuFour, & Eaker, 2008.

Figure 5.1: The PLC structure.

Systems are in place to meet the needs of students supported by the four pillars, yet some teachers are unclear on what to do in their team meetings. Highly functioning teams operate under a model of collective responsibility because they understand, as John Ross, Anne Hogaboam-Gray, and Peter Gray (2004) state, "The influence of the collective on the individual is likely to be higher in schools in which teachers share a common vision" (p. 167). All team members understand that they have an active role on the team because they collectively believe that "the whole is greater than the sum of its parts" (Dubois, 1890, p. 8).

Teams that function as PLCs understand the importance of relying on one another to achieve the mission of ensuring high levels of student learning, and as Harvard professor Richard Elmore describes in a 2002 review of research by the Albert Shanker Institute, "Accountability must be a reciprocal process. For every increment of performance I demand from you, I have an equal responsibility to provide you with the capacity to that expectation" (p. 5). Team members understand that just as they receive ideas, resources, and support from colleagues, it is their equal responsibility to provide the same when called on. They engage in open dialogue, rather than monologue from the team leader, and maintain the focus of this life-changing work around the four critical questions of a PLC.

True PLCs have collectively committed to the four critical questions. Much as the captain of an aircraft carrier uses a magnetic compass to get directions for the voyage, teams use the four critical questions as their moral compass for student learning. As shown in figure 5.2, these questions serve to orient the work of the team to maintain an effective direction on the course to their destination.

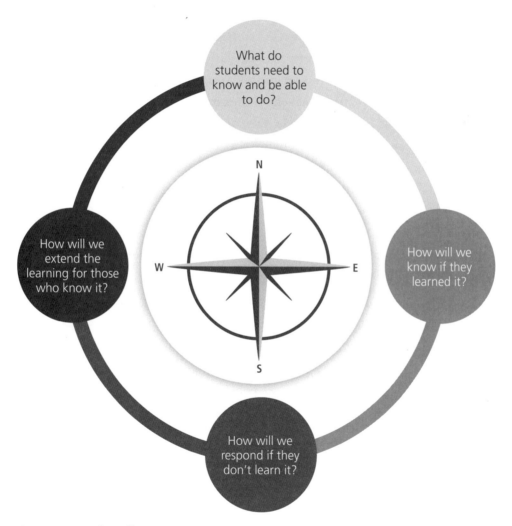

Source: © 2018 by Will Remmert.

Figure 5.2: Four critical questions of a PLC.

In his presentations at the PLC institutes and in his DVD *Are We a Group or a Team?* (2014), Mike Mattos frequently challenges educators across the world to reflect on the current effectiveness of their collaborative teams. He asks them to self-assess themselves along a continuum of one through ten, with ten being a true PLC, five being what Reeves and DuFour (2016) refer to as *PLC lite*, and one being the long-supported and traditional structure of schools in which teachers function as independent contractors within the four walls of their personal classrooms. These teachers have zero accountability to one another or student learning for all.

During the self-reflection process, educators feel comfortable choosing a number between five and ten, such as seven, because they will admit that they aren't to the level of a ten, or a true PLC, but are confident they are functioning better than a five. However, Mattos (2014) challenges educators to position their team in one of the three options he provides: one, five, or ten. The challenge comes when he requires participants to stick to the numbers of one, five, or ten rather than attempting to exist in the fictional chasms between one and five, or five and ten. Teams cannot be a three or a seven because then they are picking and choosing individual components of what they view as important to the PLC process and fail to commit to the critical aspects of working as a PLC. This activity helps solidify the work of collaborative teams and how critical the PLC process is to ensuring high levels of learning for all students.

In their book *Cultures Built to Last*, Richard DuFour and Michael Fullan (2013) reference the work of John P. Kotter and Dan S. Cohen (2002) when describing the difficulty of shifting from a traditional school structure to one that functions as a PLC. They state, "The central challenge of a systemic change is getting people to act in new ways" (as cited in DuFour & Fullan, 2013, p. 26). Moving from a one to a five requires both individual and collective commitments.

In the scenario that begins this chapter, Ms. Martinez and the first-grade team find themselves at a one because they insist on simply covering material provided in their basal series, regardless of any evidence of student learning. These teachers aren't collectively invested in ensuring the learning of their students; rather, they are working individually to ensure they are teaching the materials they have been provided. When educators function as a PLC, they understand and make the critical shift from the basic presentation of material, or teaching content, to ensuring the learning of all their students in first grade, regardless of the teacher they were assigned.

On the other hand, Mrs. Smith and the third-grade team exist in PLC purgatory, or a five on the continuum, drifting in and out of quality practices and collective responsibility, picking and choosing what practices they are most interested in committing to. DuFour (2003) would describe the fives as "collaboration lite, put[ting] student achievement on a starvation diet" (p. 63). The third-grade team members aren't fully committed to one another or the learning of all students. They may appear to be functioning well because they get along and rarely disagree about anything, but they haven't truly invested in the strengths of one another, nor do they hold one another accountable for the benefit of team growth or student learning. They are approaching the work of a collaborative team but only when it's convenient or when it won't make their colleagues uncomfortable.

Meanwhile, true PLCs are located at a ten on the continuum because they commit to clarity in roles and actions, use the four critical questions as the moral compass to navigate their day-to-day work, and are collectively engaged in a commitment to their own professional learning to achieve competence as a team.

Educators are engaged in life-altering work and must understand the significance of their impact on the students and colleagues they work with. On a much grander level, educators must commit to a vision of the future they are constructing through their intended and unintended actions because they are leaving a generational legacy. Every team, in every school, experiences struggles at one point or another. Improving the system requires educators to collectively reflect to examine their current reality from that broader generational perspective. Researcher and systems expert Donella H. Meadows (2008) states:

> Change comes first from stepping outside the limited information that can be seen from any single place in the system and getting an overview. From a wider perspective, information flows, goals, incentives, and disincentives can be restructured so that separate, bounded, rational actions do add up to results that everyone desires. (p. 108)

Teams within a school must continually reassess their impact within the system and how they can continue to help the system improve. The following section addresses a few commonly asked questions to assist teams in finding clarity and becoming competent in the life-changing work of ensuring students learn at high levels.

Common Questions About Working Together in a PLC

Following are the answers to common questions teams might ask regarding what it means to work as collaborative teams within a PLC.

Do All Teams in a PLC Have to Teach the Same Things in the Same Way?

Researchers Anthony Bryk, Louis Gomez, Alicia Grunow, and Paul LeMahieu (2015) support the need for teachers to work as professionals by collaborating with one another to determine what is critical for all students to know, because the "complexity of teaching and learning is real, and it cannot be sidestepped by standardizing all activity in an effort to 'teacher-proof' instructional environments" (pp. 186–187).

With the advent of the standardization era in education with the passage of No Child Left Behind (NCLB) in 2001, school systems have required well-educated and experienced education professionals to follow what author and education journalist John Merrow (2017) describes as "teacher-proof curricula" (p. xxxvi), such as scripted textbooks and purchased programs. This requirement compels them, through external and internal pressures, to function as amateurs. While these packaged resources certainly provide ample material for teachers and may be appropriate for some students, they typically aren't aligned to state standards or the needs of local districts, schools, and teachers; and they most certainly aren't aligned to the needs of individual students.

When we function in a PLC, we understand that some aspects of our practice are tight and some are loose. The first critical question—What do students need to know and be able to do?—focuses teams to find coherence by collectively determining what is essential for every student to learn in the present grade level or content area. This is the *tight* aspect. The *loose* aspect of the first critical question is the methods, materials, or strategies individual teachers use to ensure their students have mastered these essentials.

In a PLC, schools treat teachers as professionals, and teachers have the flexibility to determine the best methods to ensure all students are learning at high levels. This is supported with data as the evidence of learning. This is the balance in what Robert Marzano (2010) describes as the art and science of teaching. The art is allowing individual educators to creatively design and deliver lessons, guided by the team-determined essential standards, to most effectively meet the needs of all students. The science comes through collective data analysis to determine which practices are most effective, which is the second critical question of a PLC—How will we know if they learned it?

If your team is struggling with what is tight and loose, we suggest the following three-step activity.

1. As a team, determine an essential concept or skill to teach in the next week. (tight)

2. Individually, using a piece of paper, briefly describe the strategies and resources you will be utilizing to deliver the lesson. (loose)

3. As a team, openly and honestly compare what team members developed, discussing the pros and cons of the proposed plans. Include a common time frame when you will implement the lesson.

This activity is a simple way to begin exploring what is tight and loose, as well as taking teams to a higher level of collaboration. Once you complete this activity, the next step in the process is to determine the effectiveness of the lesson to ensure student learning. Use the following four-step activity to continue the learning process.

1. After completing the first activity, as a team, develop a short three- to five-question common formative assessment that you will administer to all students to determine the effectiveness of the lesson. (tight)

2. Individually collect the data and bring the results to the next team meeting. (tight)

3. Collectively share the results, and review the differences between results and strategies (tight) as well as the resources utilized across the team. (loose)

4. Determine which strategies and resources teachers used were the most effective to ensure student learning. Then begin planning how to use those strategies to respond to students who have yet to master the essential standards. (tight)

Why Do Team Members Need to Share Students?

Critical questions 3 and 4 are opportunities to better meet the needs of all students, not just those who haven't quite mastered the content but also those whom we can push into deeper learning. While educators want to be everything for every student, every minute of every day, the reality is much more complex.

It is impossible for individual teachers to meet the needs of every student, during every lesson, every day; we must work collaboratively to give all students their best opportunity to master the essentials.

The following place, analyze, redistribute (PAR) activity and template (see figure 5.3) provides a straightforward example of how teams can share the load across a grade level or content area.

- **Place:** Identify the needs of individual students.

- **Analyze:** Analyze areas that teams need to address.

- **Redistribute:** Decide which team member is best suited to intervene with the students who need the most support based on CFA results.

Target	Students Who Need More Time and Support	Students Who Would Benefit From More Practice	Students Who Would Benefit From Enrichment or Extension
Target One			
Target Two			
Target Three			
Target Four			

Figure 5.3: PAR activity template.

*Visit **go.SolutionTree.com/PLCbooks** for a free reproducible version of this figure.*

Have the team complete the following five-step PAR activity.

1. After administering a short three- to five-question CFA, individual teachers *place* students in the appropriate location on the template.

    o **Students who need more time and support:** These students have significant gaps in their understanding of the target and need intensive support.

    o **Students who would benefit from more practice:** These students are those who may have made minor errors or perhaps need a little more reinforcement of the target, not necessarily a full reteaching opportunity.

○ **Students who would benefit from enrichment or extension:** These students have full understanding and would benefit from deeper learning.

2. The team members come together with their individual templates completed.

3. The team *analyzes* the individual forms and begins placing all students across the team into the appropriate areas on a master team document.

4. The team plans how to collectively respond to all students, including which teacher is best suited to support the students who need it most, based on individual results.

5. The team then *redistributes* students to work with the appropriate team members, as identified in the previous step, for intervention or extension.

What Do Team Members Do If They Disagree About the Right Work?

Schools that engage in the work of PLCs consist of collaborative teams working interdependently to best meet the wide-ranging needs of all students. This challenging yet exciting work brings together the backgrounds, hopes and dreams, successes and failures, personalities, and years of experience of different people, with a goal of educators uniting to collectively function as one heart and mind. Inevitably, differences of philosophy and opinion can create conflict and tension within teams. When teams experience disagreement, it is critical for team members to understand their colleagues' perspectives.

Collaborative teams can use the following seven-step, four-pillar activity to discuss the focus of their work as well as their individual and collective commitments. This activity assists teams to identify and address individual perspectives within their team in a safe and supportive format. When differences appear across the four pillars, team members listen to one another for understanding and work to reach consensus about next steps to move forward.

1. Individually and *honestly*, each team member reflects on his or her current reality around the four pillars, using the chart in figure 5.4 (page 84).

The PLC Structure

The work of a PLC is united through interdependent collaborative teams of professionals working to ensure high levels of learning for all students. These collaborative teams build on the foundation of a PLC by uniting their beliefs and practices and developing structures around the four pillars.

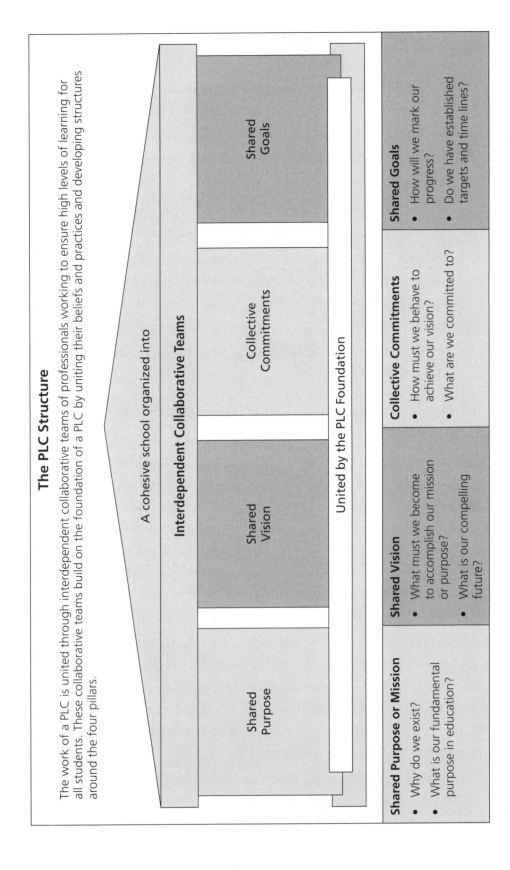

A cohesive school organized into

Interdependent Collaborative Teams

Shared Purpose

Shared Vision

Collective Commitments

Shared Goals

United by the PLC Foundation

Shared Purpose or Mission
- Why do we exist?
- What is our fundamental purpose in education?

Shared Vision
- What must we become to accomplish our mission or purpose?
- What is our compelling future?

Collective Commitments
- How must we behave to achieve our vision?
- What are we committed to?

Shared Goals
- How will we mark our progress?
- Do we have established targets and time lines?

Examples

1 = I became a teacher to teach.

5 = I believe most students can learn and will give my best individual effort.

10 = All students will learn at high levels, and I'm committed to working interdependently to do everything possible to make it happen.

Individual			Team		
1	5	10	1	5	10

Examples

1 = Some students will learn, and some will not.

5 = Seventy percent proficiency is really good. Can we really get all students to learn at high levels?

10 = We will work together to ensure all students have everything they need to succeed beyond high school.

Individual			Team		
1	5	10	1	5	10

Examples

1 = I have so much to prepare, I don't have time for more meetings.

5 = I get to all the meetings, but I'm not always prepared or on time.

10 = We have established team norms and hold one another accountable because our students need our very best every day.

Individual			Team		
1	5	10	1	5	10

Examples

1 = My measurement is whatever is in my gradebook.

5 = We set SMART goals at the beginning of the year but don't really revisit them until the end of the year (O'Neill & Conzemius, 2013).

10 = We are dedicated to ensuring all students master the essential standards and continually monitor progress and adjust practices throughout the year.

Individual			Team		
1	5	10	1	5	10

Directions: Independently and honestly, reflect on the current reality of the four pillars for your team, first as an individual. Then reflect and assess your team commitment to the four pillars. When completed, post your individual and team scores on chart paper and engage in dialogue around areas of commonality and areas for growth as a team.

Note: Scores can only be a 1, 5, or 10.

Source: Adapted from DuFour et al., 2016.

Figure 5.4: The PLC structure.

Visit go.SolutionTree.com/PLCbooks for a free reproducible version of this figure.

2. Each team member then reflects on his or her actions and how they impact the team. Team members circle their score as a one, five, or ten for each of the four pillars.

3. Team members then individually assess the commitment of the team and circle their score as a one, five, or ten for each of the four pillars.

4. After individual self-assessment, team members use chart paper or a whiteboard to collectively post the individual and team scores.

5. As a group, team members begin identifying areas of commonality and strengths as well as areas for growth. One team member can serve as the scribe.

6. The team ensures that everyone has had a chance to speak and be heard, and recognizes and values everyone's views.

7. The team uses the data and notes to begin developing a plan.

    o What areas should teachers celebrate?

    o What is the team improvement plan?

    o What commitments does the team need from individual members to move forward?

    o What does the team need to do to move forward to becoming a ten?

What Is the Purpose for Creating an Action Plan?

Three big ideas drive the work of a PLC, and teams should be sure action plans align directly to these ideas. DuFour et al. (2016) outline these three big ideas as follows.

1. A focus on learning

2. A collaborative culture and collective responsibility

3. A results orientation

Utilizing an action plan helps create clarity, consistency, alignment, and support, leading to competence for the entire team and the school system, with school district goals, building goals, and team goals. An effective action plan aligns the three big ideas in one document, serving as a guide for teachers to provide evidence of their collaboration around student learning and supporting it with results. Teams can start by doing the following four steps.

1. Establish expectations and norms for team behaviors. Teams purposefully revisit these norms to ensure team members address them regularly and abide by them at team meetings.

2. Distribute leadership and accountability throughout the collaborative team to ensure everyone has an active role in the team process. Roles and responsibilities within the team may include some or all of the following.

   ○ **Team leader:** Coordinates team agendas and serves as the official voice of the team

   ○ **Scribe:** Keeps track of discussions and is in charge of following through with documentation and updating data within the action plan

   ○ **Timekeeper:** Monitors time to ensure the team stays on task, making efficient and effective use of the time provided; frequently serves in the unofficial role of upholding the team norms regarding time

   ○ **Planner:** May work with external members of the team or school to coordinate events such as assessment dates

   ○ **Investigator:** Dives into research and data to support the work of the team or further investigate opportunities to better meet student needs

3. Align teamwork to building and district goals to help create a results orientation across teams, the building, and the district. With SMART goals displayed prominently, individual teams better understand the importance of their collaborative efforts toward achieving goals for all students across the system (O'Neill & Conzemius, 2013). Through unified and interdependent alignment, focused on student learning, teams gain better clarity on where they are going and how they are accountable to an aligned vision of the system.

4. Create a running record of team actions, driven by data and guided by the moral compass of the four critical questions, to help teams become interdependently accountable, providing insight of team functionality.

Highly functioning schools create systems that prioritize interdependence, where faculty share a collective responsibility for every student. When the action plan (figure 5.5, page 88) is available and transparent to external members of the core

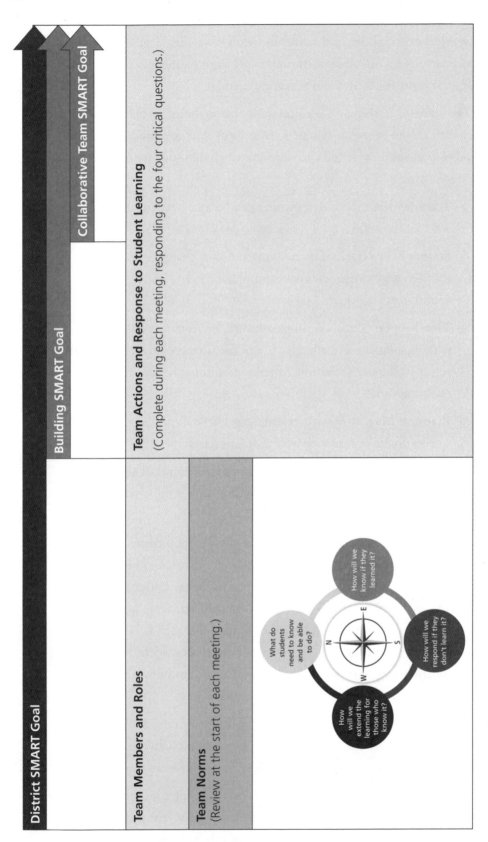

Source: © 2018 by Will Remmert.

Figure 5.5: Team action plan.

Visit go.SolutionTree.com/PLCbooks for a free reproducible version of this figure.

collaborative team, such as instructional coaches, specialists, or building administration, they assume ownership of every student and no longer refer to students as *mine*; rather, they say *ours*.

These effective schools make team action plans available in shared and confidential spaces such as conference rooms or through formats such as Google Docs. Offering the action plan to other professionals in the building opens the door to collaboration, allowing for more effective and efficient alignment and providing schoolwide support for teams and students that need it.

The following eight-step activity helps teams create an effective action plan.

1. At a staff meeting with all teams present, utilize four sheets of chart paper and title each one as follows.

    a. Goals

    b. Roles and Responsibilities

    c. Norms

    d. Actions

2. Divide each chart in half with one half representing current reality and the other half representing future orientation.

3. On the Goals sheet, indicate the current reality of the district, building, and team goals and how they are currently aligned, monitored, and adjusted over time. Indicate future steps to bring alignment across the system, including brainstorming improvements in accountability.

4. On the Roles and Responsibilities sheet, indicate how you currently distribute roles across team members. Discuss and record improvements for moving forward to provide clarity and investment of everyone on the team.

5. On the Norms sheet, record the teams' current norms on one side of the chart, engage in dialogue around the collective commitments the team members are making to one another moving forward, and then record those results on the other side.

6. On the Actions sheet, list the current reality of how teams record and monitor actions and responses to student learning across the system to provide clarity and transparency. Develop ideas for how to move

forward to provide more interdependence and reciprocal accountability across teams, the building, and the district.

7. Post the individual team charts throughout the meeting area and conduct a gallery walk for others to learn from one another and add to their own learning. Participants should take individual notes to determine what aligns with their thinking and new ideas moving forward.

8. Teams reconvene to reflect on their new learning, adjusting the work they created and agreeing on steps to move forward as a team and as a school.

How to Coach Your Team

Supporting and coaching teams in the PLC process is critical for success. Following are five tips for team leaders and coaches to help provide the clarity and support needed to achieve that success.

1. Leaders must engage in dialogue with teams about what is critical with the current task. They should ask clarifying questions to help guide the team to ensure their work around the four pillars, four critical questions, or three big ideas of a PLC is aligned with their mission and vision.

2. Educators frequently take on too many items at once, losing focus of what is essential for students to learn. Leaders must maintain high expectations for the team and student learning; however, they must also provide safe spaces, while providing permission for educators to let some things go, identify areas that take precedent, take calculated risks for student learning, and trust the judgment of the professionals who will find the most effective method to meet student needs. Leaders must also work with teams to analyze and reflect on the data, develop conclusions, and construct next steps.

3. Maintaining a balance of what is tight and what is loose will help provide clarity for teams. Leaders must establish and communicate a clear understanding of expectations while allowing teachers the professional flexibility to meet those expectations. If teams aren't meeting those expectations, leaders must reflect on those communications and then reinvest and recommunicate to ensure clarity leads to competence.

4. Leaders must develop structures for teams to support one another through sharing action plans and data. An avenue for this transparency is effectively utilizing regularly scheduled meetings to share this information. These meetings begin to function as another collaborative team within the building, in which staff share successes and challenges with their colleagues in a vertical or cross-departmental manner, providing perspective and clarity.

5. A critical step for any team is to return to the four critical questions and use those as its moral compass to assist in directing team members toward their destination. The four questions provide clarity and lead the team toward competence and high levels of student learning.

Conclusion

This chapter began with a common scenario experienced by teams and schools across the globe. While your current reality may not be identical to this scenario, yours likely has similarities. There is no magic formula to move forward, but maintaining a laser-like focus on the key foundation of a PLC will move your team to greater levels of student learning. As legendary basketball coach John Wooden stated, "Little things make big things happen" (Wooden & Jamison, 2005, p. 135).

When confronted with a challenge, we should remember Schmoker's (2004) quote from the epigraph of this chapter, which Rebecca DuFour emphasized throughout her career educating teams of teachers, that "clarity precedes competence." Because the day-to-day work of a teacher is layered with what feels like an infinite number of tasks, it is understandable that teams can become disoriented. During these times, it is critical to realign team commitments to the four critical questions, serving as a moral compass to orient the work of collaborative teams to ensuring student learning.

Additional Resources

Teams can use these helpful resources to gain further guidance and insights for their collaborative work.

- **AllThingsPLC.info:** This website has everything educators, teams, schools, and districts need to move forward in the PLC process. Simply refining your search by school size, configuration, or demographics can help you locate a situation similar to yours and how this PLC effectively ensured higher levels of learning for all students.

- ***Focus: Elevating the Essentials to Radically Improve Student Learning* (2nd ed.):** This book by Mike Schmoker (2018) supports the work of PLCs by assisting educators in maintaining their attention on the critical pieces of student learning.

- ***Simplifying Response to Intervention: Four Essential Guiding Principles*:** This 2012 book by Buffum et al. pulls together the PLC and RTI core concepts to guide schools in the work of ensuring students learn what is essential and providing them certain access to that learning.

6

Changing to a Positive School Culture

A bad system will beat a good person every time.

—W. Edwards Deming

The Story of Barnestown Middle School

"Let's put the *fun* in *dysfunctional*" was basically the motto of Barnestown Middle School, one of the lowest-achieving schools in the state. When the school hired its current principal, the superintendent told him, "I don't really care about improving academics at that school; it's already a lost cause. Just fix the staff; they are a mess and highly dysfunctional." The new principal replied, "Let's fix both."

The new principal has heard many stories about the school and the dysfunctional staff, considering he previously was an assistant principal at the high school the middle school feeds into. Since he has heard so many stories, he feels that he needs to go in with a very open mind and give everyone a voice and a chance. He also decides to implement the PLC process.

The principal meets with the previously established leadership team, listens to its concerns, and finds some very well-intentioned staff members who truly believe all students could learn. They mention the dysfunction, of course, but during this first meeting, the principal's intent is to understand the pulse of the school.

The leadership decides it would be a great idea to kick off the year with a staff retreat to a large restaurant that also includes an arcade. The staff thought that team-building activities and friendly competition might help bring everyone together. The new principal is on board, as long as the leadership team agrees to spend the first half of the day providing professional development around the foundational pieces of the PLC process. The principal is careful never to utter the words *professional learning community* because he knows that some staff might think this is just something else the district is making them do and "this too would pass."

The principal asks the leadership team if anyone can share the school's mission, vision, collective commitments, and goals. Not one person can provide an answer. It is clear that he should begin the PLC process by focusing on the foundational pieces of a PLC at the retreat.

The leadership team retreat begins with the development of a new mission statement for the school.

Our school will provide a positive, safe, and caring educational environment that promotes student learning, responsibility, and diversity.

We will accomplish this by:

- Modeling excellent behavior

- Applying content standards to guide student learning

- Helping students make real-life connections

- Collaborating and communicating with all stakeholders

Even though the principal knows the mission statement still needs work, this process has opened his eyes to the fact that his teachers are good educators who understand that student learning is their purpose. He also realizes that some teachers have just forgotten how to stay focused on student learning, others have implicit bias toward a changing demographic, and others have been influenced for a long time by a few strong negative voices. All in all, he has hope.

The next step is to create a new vision statement for the school. After an hour of highly professional conversation, the staff come up with the following vision: "We will meet or exceed our adequate yearly progress (AYP), and we will reach effective status within one year and excellent status within three years."

Once again, the new principal is starting to see that the staff really do want to improve.

The next step is for the staff to develop collective commitments and values that will guide the actions of the team throughout the school year. The principal asks the staff to consider the following three questions.

1. What promises are you willing to make to your colleagues that will support our success in achieving our mission and vision?

2. When your students leave you, how do you want them to be different, as people, as a result of being with you all year long?

3. What are your fundamental, bedrock beliefs about your role in making sure all students learn at high levels?

The following is a summary of what the teachers write about their collective commitments.

-   We will be flexible, professional, respectful, encouraging, creative, caring, supportive, dedicated, and willing to go the extra mile.

-   We will be open and honest, empathetic, and understanding lifelong learners.

-   We will be open to the community, unbiased, fair, nonjudgmental, and open minded.

-   We will put students first and be student focused; celebrate and educate our students and each other; and be enthusiastic, positive, and motivated.

-   We will protect instructional time.

-   We will respect everyone's level of expertise.

-   We will have smiles and teach smiles.

-   We will support a safe and consistent, orderly learning environment.

Once again, the new principal feels a glimmer of hope with the heartfelt responses from his staff.

Now it is getting close to lunch, and incredibly, the staff have created a new mission statement, a vision statement, and their collective commitments, all in a short, focused three hours of time. They decide not to establish specific goals until the state department releases the state scores for each school. But since the leadership team members know that they would most likely be in the bottom 5 percent of the state, they decide to start with two very general goals aligned to their vision.

1. Increase academic achievement.

2. Close the achievement gap by meeting or exceeding AYP.

After lunch, the staff participate in team building by playing arcade games in the restaurant. Many teachers share that this is the first time they have ever gotten together as a group in the past fifteen years. The new principal can sense the excitement and feels good about getting the foundational parts of the PLC process established and in place. The key is to keep the focus and live the mission, vision, collective commitments, and goals.

Following the retreat, the leadership team makes posters of the mission, vision, collective commitments, and goals and posts them in the school lobby for everyone to see as soon as they walk through the door each morning. The team even posts the collective commitments exactly how the staff have written them on sticky notes and laminates over them to hold them in place.

The majority of the staff commit to the PLC process even though they actually have no idea that's what they are doing. Over the years, the school moves teachers into both interdisciplinary and departmental teams and gives them more than forty minutes of collaboration time each day. They use this collaboration time to create and analyze common assessments and drive instruction. Within a six-year period, the school becomes the highest-achieving urban, high-poverty school in Ohio.

During that same time, almost half the staff turns over. Many teachers find out that they do not truly believe that all students could learn, and this school is not the place for them because it takes a lot of hard, focused work to meet all students' needs. While many leave, others receive promotions. Seven former teachers become district-level administrators or principals. By laying the PLC foundation right away and focusing on the right work, this school is able to change the culture from dysfunctional to highly functional in a few years.

This work at Barnestown Middle School was not easy, and the staff and principal worked tirelessly to make sure they were meeting the needs of all students. They started with laying the foundation of the PLC process and created buy-in to embrace the cultural shifts and changes that were needed to move this school forward. This chapter focuses on helping teams create a school culture that embraces positive change, one in which teams can collaborate to support each other and their students to achieve at the highest levels.

What the Experts Say

Culture is powerful. It has a significant influence on everything that happens in a school: how the staff dress, what they discuss, how willing they might be to change, their instructional practices, and the importance of teacher and student learning (Deal & Peterson, 1994; Firestone & Wilson, 1985; Newmann, 1996).

School leaders often use *climate* and *culture* interchangeably. However, the literature differentiates these interrelated concepts in important ways. *Climate* describes the shared perceptions of the people in a group or organization, while *culture* includes how people feel about the organization and the beliefs, values, and assumptions that provide the identity and set the standards of behavior (Stolp & Smith, 1995).

Culture is truly about what people believe and value. In order for a school to be a place that provides high levels of learning for all students, regardless of student background, the staff must articulate the following through their behavior and beliefs (DuFour et al., 2008; DuFour & Eaker, 1998).

- All students can learn.

- All students will learn because of what we do.

"School culture is the set of norms, values and beliefs, rituals and ceremonies, symbols, and stories that make up the 'persona' of the school," says Kent D. Peterson (1998), a professor in the Department of Educational Administration at the University of Wisconsin–Madison.

Schools that demonstrate a positive culture have:

1. A shared sense of purpose, where they pour their hearts into teaching

2. Underlying norms of collegiality, improvement, and hard work

3. Rituals and traditions celebrating student accomplishment, teacher innovation, and parental commitment

4. Informal network of storytellers, heroes, and heroines that provide a social web of information, support, and history

5. Success, joy, and humor (Peterson & Deal, 1998, p. 29)

Schools with a solid, positive culture have a strong foundation. The culture of a PLC starts with a commitment to a shared mission, a vision, collective commitments, and goals that the staff create together. These foundational parts of the PLC process are extremely important because they represent our purpose, future, values, and beliefs and our focus on results.

We have worked with thousands of educators over the years and have never met any teacher who got into the profession for the wrong reasons. These teachers didn't get into the profession because they don't like students or don't want them to be successful. Every educator got into the profession because he or she wanted to help students grow. For whatever reason, many educators have lost that core belief or value, and we need to help them find that core value again.

Terrence E. Deal and Kent D. Peterson (1994) share that school leaders do the following seven things to shape a positive culture.

1. Communicate core values in what they say and do.

2. Honor and recognize those who have worked to serve the students and the purpose of the school.

3. Observe rituals and traditions to support the school's heart and soul.

4. Recognize heroes and heroines and the work these exemplars accomplish.

5. Speak eloquently of the deeper mission of the school.

6. Celebrate the accomplishments of the staff, students, and community.

7. Preserve the focus on students by recounting stories of success and achievement.

Deal and Peterson (1998) explain that in toxic cultures, staff view students as the problem rather than as their valued clients. Staff are sometimes part of negative subcultures that are hostile and critical of change. Many staff believe they are doing the best they can and don't search out new ideas.

There are many stories and historical perspectives on a school that are often negative, discouraging, and demoralizing. The same people tend to complain, criticize, and distrust any new ideas, approaches, or suggestions for improvement raised by planning committees. They also rarely share ideas, materials, or solutions to classroom problems and rarely participate in ceremonies or school traditions that celebrate what is good and hopeful about their school.

What is school culture, and who shapes it? Culture is the underground stream of norms, values, beliefs, traditions, and rituals that has built up over time as people work together, solve problems, and confront challenges. This set of informal expectations and values shapes how people think, feel, and act in schools. This highly enduring web of influence binds the school together and makes it special. It is up to school leaders—principals, teachers, and often families—to help identify, shape, and maintain strong, positive, student-focused school cultures. Without these supportive cultures, reforms will wither, and student learning will slip (Deal & Peterson, 1998).

Common Questions About Changing School Culture

Following are the answers to common questions teams might ask about making the necessary changes to ensure your school culture is focused on student learning.

How Do Teams Create a Strong Culture for Learning?

We suggest starting your journey through the culture change of a PLC by focusing on the foundation. Begin by taking the time to develop a shared mission, a vision, collective commitments, and goals. You can use the following activities to help work toward your strong foundation.

Mission Activity

1. Teams of teachers work together with markers and chart paper, and write the primary purpose of the school and how they will achieve that purpose.

2. Teams switch papers with another group and add anything they think would help identify the purpose and how they will achieve that purpose.

3. After several rotations, the teams then combine all the comments into one document.

4. After reflection and processing, teams can refine the document.

Vision Activity

1. Teams of teachers work together with markers and chart paper, and write what they want their school to be like in the future. What do they want their school to become?

2. Teams switch papers with another group and add anything they think would help identify the vision and how they will achieve that vision.

3. After several rotations, the teams then combine all the comments into one document.

4. After reflection and processing, teams can refine the document.

Collective Commitments Activity

1. Start with three sheets of chart paper, with one statement at the top of each page.

   a. **Statement 1:** What promises are you willing to make to your colleagues that will support our success in achieving our mission and vision?

   b. **Statement 2:** When your students leave you, how do you want them to be different, as people, as a result of being with you all year long?

   c. **Statement 3:** What are your fundamental, bedrock beliefs about your role in making sure all students learn at high levels?

2. Have every staff member in the school write his or her answer to each question on a sticky note. If people have more than one answer for each question, they can write them on separate sticky notes.

3. You can complete this activity in thirty minutes. Each year, as new staff members come on board, they can add their answers.

Goals Activity

1. To complete this activity, the staff must first have an understanding of SMART goals. SMART goals must be (O'Neill & Conzemius, 2013):

   ○ **S**—Specific

   ○ **M**—Measurable

   ○ **A**—Attainable

   ○ **R**—Results oriented

   ○ **T**—Time bound

2. Provide each team with examples of SMART goals and non-SMART goals so teams can compare and contrast the differences.

3. Teams then decide what goals they will focus on. Remember, less is more.

4. Once teams have an understanding of SMART goals, they can align their goals to the building goals, which should in turn align to the district goals.

How Do Teams Determine Their Current Reality?

To get a good view of your school's current reality, you must understand the six characteristics of a PLC. These six characteristics would be the same for all high-performing schools.

1. Shared mission, vision, values, and goals

2. Collective inquiry

3. Collaborative culture

4. Action orientation and experimentation

5. Continuous improvement

6. Focus on results

The following activity can help schools determine their current reality. We suggest using this activity at least three times per year (beginning, middle, and end).

1. Write the six characteristics of a PLC on separate sheets of chart paper.

   a. Shared mission, vision, values, and goals

   b. Collective inquiry

   c. Collaborative culture

   d. Action orientation and experimentation

   e. Continuous improvement

   f. Focus on results

2. Under each characteristic, make a number line from one to ten. One means that this is not happening, and ten means your team is already doing this and is a model for the rest of the school.

3. Define each characteristic and discuss each one with staff.

4. Ask teachers to mark where they feel they or their teams rank on the number line for each characteristic.

5. After they all have placed their marks, have teams address *what, so what,* and *now what* about the activity. Have them write *what* they feel

and understand about the information gathered; *so what* is what they can learn from this, and *now what* are the next steps moving forward. Complete this activity each quarter to see how each team is progressing.

How Do Teams Address Dysfunctional Behavior?

There are many types of behavior people may describe as dysfunctional, especially when working in a low-achieving school. First, we must always assume positive intentions and listen to understand instead of listening to plan what we are going to say next. DuFour et al. (2016) claim that "another powerful lever for changing behavior is the positive peer pressure and support that come with being a team member" (p. 148).

Sometimes in low-achieving schools, the facts are there but no one is willing to change, so you have to start to focus on positive peer pressure. For example, at Barnestown Middle School, there was an eighth-grade science team with three teachers; one had been in the building for twenty-five years, and the two others were fairly new. The team's test scores were always below 30 percent until the two new teachers started using common formative assessments aligned to learning targets to monitor their students' progress. Suddenly, their scores skyrocketed to over 80 percent. The teacher who had been doing the same thing for twenty-five years and getting the same bad results finally asked the other two teachers what they were doing. The young teachers were very excited that this veteran had finally asked for their help and assistance. The older teacher started to implement common formative assessments like the other two, and his results increased dramatically. This veteran had basically given up until the positive peer pressure of others' success drove him to want to improve his own results. This is a fairly common story. We should always be open to learning from each other.

How to Coach Your Team

How do schools deal with toxicity in their culture? Deal and Peterson (1998) suggest several things educators can do. These include the following:

- Confront negativity and hostility head-on and work to redirect negative energies.

- Protect emergent sources of positive focus and effort.

- Actively recruit more positive and constructive staff.

- Vigorously celebrate the positive and the improving sides of the school.

- Ensure that improvement efforts and plans are successful by supporting them with time, energy, and resources.

- Reconnect staff to the mission of schools: To help all children learn and grow.

Without positive, supportive school cultures, reforms will inevitably fail to take root, staff morale and commitment will falter, and student learning will continue to decrease.

Conclusion

It is imperative for all educators to understand that schools must ensure learning for all students. We would go a step further and say that we have to ensure learning for every *person* in the school and community, including students, staff, families, and community members. We must collectively develop as a school and articulate our mission and vision to the entire school community. We must create and own our collective responsibilities and commitments to make sure we are doing what we have a moral obligation to do, which is to make sure all students learn at high levels.

Additional Resources

Teams can use these helpful resources to gain further guidance and insights for their collaborative work.

- *Transforming School Culture: How to Overcome Staff Division*: In this second edition, Anthony Muhammad (2017) provides a school improvement plan for leaders to overcome staff division, improve staff relationships, and change toxic school cultures into positive ones.

- *School Improvement for All: A How-To Guide for Doing the Right Work*: In this practical guide, Sharon V. Kramer and Sarah Schuhl (2017) help K–12 educators use the PLC at Work process to drive continuous school improvement and support student success. Target your school's specific needs with an immediate course of action for improving school culture and performance.

- *Cultures Built to Last: Systemic PLCs at Work*: In this book, DuFour and Fullan (2013) help take your PLC to the next level. Discover a systemwide approach for re-envisioning your PLC while sustaining growth and continuing momentum.

Involving Nondepartmental
Members in a PLC

Traveller, there's no path. Paths are made by walking.

—Antonio Machado

The Story of Johnstone High School

Johnstone High School (JHS) has been on the PLC journey for ten years. By all accounts, most staff members would agree that they have addressed the basic tenets of the process. Their mission and vision focus on helping all students learn at high levels. They have collaborative teams firmly established and have specific weekly meeting times with required attendance. All meetings have an agenda, which lists the four critical questions of a PLC at the top, facilitative roles that rotate, and meeting norms at the bottom of the agenda. Each team produces a written document that it shares with the team, department, and administration. This document lists what team members accomplished and has agenda items for the next meeting.

All departments have established norms that they attempt to follow, and some even have developed unique ways to handle norm violations. Not only do departments celebrate together both personally and professionally, but the school also celebrates monthly the accomplishments of staff and students, especially when they reach their goals. Johnstone High School is a positive place where teachers and administrators work together to help each other and the students succeed.

In addition to a positive culture of learning, JHS is focused on results. Teams have common assessments, formative assessments, and summative assessments that they administer on a regular basis. The data they review create rich discussions teams use to establish a clear picture of not only students' strengths and areas for growth but also the teachers'. Because there is weekly RTI time built into the master schedule, the teams divide students into three categories based on assessment data: (1) those who have mastered the standard, (2) those who are approaching mastery, and (3) those who have not yet met the standard. Teams then plan interventions or extension activities according to the number of students in each category. They share this information with their departments and with the administrator who oversees that department.

Johnstone High School has collaborative and RTI time built into the weekly schedule. In fact, the principal has figured out, via the master schedule, a way to allow many teams to have common prep time, allowing for further collaborative time within the workday.

For the past several years, there has been a growing underlying tension at the high school related to who actually should be participating in team and department meetings. More specifically, there is confusion around why nondepartmental faculty (or members) need to join or even attend collaborative meetings. JHS has had a long tradition of "if you teach it, you team it." While certainly everyone is collegial with each other, some teachers are confused why it is necessary (or even productive) to have outsiders be part of the collaborative process.

The general consensus at JHS is that personnel and departments not directly involved with the curricular portion of student learning can feel like a burden to the group. While teams indicate that the special education department, counseling department, psychologist, interventionists, teachers on special assignment, and nurses are incredibly valuable resources for intervention or learning development strategies for specific students, they struggle with engaging these groups around critical questions 1 and 2 of the PLC process: What do students need to know and be able to do? and How will we know if they learned it? Many have vocalized to the administration that these departments and individuals are excellent resources for the team but are not considered actual team members. The sentiment is that these colleagues should focus on their areas of expertise, such as 504s, IEPs, nuanced teaching strategies, and the RTI process.

Johnstone High School is struggling with being inclusive of all its staff. In this chapter, we will explore how to be more inclusive and how nondepartmental members can enhance both student and adult learning. Because teams are the critical component to a successful PLC, learning how to include all members is essential to ensure that a PLC is high functioning.

What the Experts Say

Most business and education experts would agree that being a third wheel can be complicated, especially when it comes to collaborating. Maybe you are the special education teacher who was assigned to meet with the English department, or the counselor who feels useless as you sit with the science team members as they work on pacing guides, or the instructional coach who understands content but is unclear as to why you need to attend the weekly mathematics team meeting.

The truth is, feeling like an outsider or being perceived as an outsider can make working in, on, and with a collaborative team very uncomfortable. This resistance to outsiders or third wheelers is predictable, and both parties feel it. The third wheel feels isolated, unwelcome, and possibly nervous about joining the team. This is normal, as it can be intimidating to join a team when you feel out of place.

Alternatively, team members may not understand why you are present. They may feel threatened and concerned about the changes a new team member may bring to the group dynamics. They may be worried about changes in alliances, or they may just feel put upon. In order for the shift from a loose affiliation of people (group) to the interdependence of a collaborative team to occur, the team must address these issues, feelings, and concerns.

In his article "4 Basic Human Needs Leaders Must Meet to Have Engaged Employees," Randy Conley (2015) talks about the need of all humans to feel engaged before work can be meaningful. The four areas of engagement include the following.

1. **Trust:** Trust is the foundation of any successful relationship, both in the classroom and during meeting times. Many will resist making themselves vulnerable if they don't feel safe or can't trust other team members.

2. **Hope:** People need to believe they will be able to grow, develop their skills, and have the opportunity to be a contributing member of

the team. It is the team's collective job to foster that hope in the overall team and the individual.

3. **Competence:** Team members' talents should align with the challenges of the work. If a team member is in over his or her head or the work is too challenging or vague, it can lead to discouragement and frustration.

4. **Sense of worth:** Despite its struggles and challenges, we derive a tremendous amount of self-worth from our work. Team members must feel confident that their hard work, commitment, and contributions will make a difference.

Moving from groups to interdependent teams cannot be forced or mandated; it must be *nurtured*. Teams must grow into interdependence through learning together and practicing together. Teams that learn together and practice their craft together are much more likely to act as an interdependent team rather than a group. In her blog *Rebels at Work*, Lois Kelly (2016) emphasizes what she calls three *change muscles* to help with this process. These include (1) *appreciation*, (2) *understanding of character strengths*, and (3) *creation of a psychologically safe environment*. She goes on to say that appreciation is one of the biggest motivators, as it builds trust, boosts confidence, and helps generate new ideas. Character strength breeds empathy, understanding, and complementary value as well as providing an understanding of the strengths of you and your coworkers. Lastly, psychological safety is very important to creating a high-performing team and a safe zone to work and learn.

In his article "3 Ways to Build Trust on Your Team," Joe Hirsch (2017) discusses how the Chicago Cubs changed their culture to build trust and, subsequently, win the World Series. In summary, he feels the three key ways to build trust are as follows.

1. **Get to know the other person:** We are taught early on never to trust strangers, and unless we intentionally grow out of that mindset, we are likely to resist others. The design of the Cubs' clubhouse encouraged players to interact with each other and therefore get to know each other better.

2. **Readily share information:** A clubhouse can quickly turn into silos as players can slip into their own personal escapes. Creating a sense of collegiality can help information pass more readily and naturally among participants, which builds trust.

3. **Facilitate whole-person growth:** The clubhouse breeds trust by putting a strong emphasis on the growth and well-being of all its players. It features a wellness lab, a mindfulness bar, and a strength and conditioning center. When teams make time for recreation and reflection, it allows for whole-person growth, which has a powerful effect on engagement.

In summary, Hirsch (2017) states that "trust is an elusive quality that doesn't come easily." By overcoming the barriers that block friendship, understanding, and progress, we can establish trust in our teams that makes them perform at the highest levels.

Common Questions About Nondepartmental Members

Following are the answers to common questions teams might ask regarding involving nondepartmental staff members in your collaborative teams and the challenges and benefits of working together.

Who Are Nondepartmental Members?

Here, the variety of professional groups we refer to as *nondepartmental members* for the sake of simplicity and clarity include special educators, counselors, interventionists, teachers on special assignment, and health care professionals.

- **Special educators:** This is a broad canopy. Special education includes psychologists, speech and language therapists, occupational therapists, physical therapists, and any other specialist on campus who works with special needs students.

- **Counselors:** This group can include academic counselors, guidance counselors, at-risk counselors, social workers, and college and career counselors.

- **Interventionists or teachers on special assignment:** This group includes teachers on special assignment or any other classroom teacher who is now working outside the classroom or directly with adult learners.

- **Health care professionals:** This group includes any health-related professionals and may overlap with special education.

What Can Nondepartmental Members Offer to an Established Team?

When you begin to design, build, and group collaborative teams with nondepartmental members, consider five primary areas of strength that will enhance any collaborative team. These five areas, coupled with Randy Conley's (2015) four basic needs for human engagement, can lead to powerful collaboration in which all staff members break down the departmental barrier for nondepartmental members.

The following are the five primary areas of strength for nondepartmental members.

1. **Academic background:** All these professionals have an undergraduate education background that is likely to match up with a content area. Many of them have advanced degrees in a specific field. For example, the special education teacher may have been an English major, the nurse may have a degree in anatomy and physiology, or the counselor might have a background in social studies.

2. **Data analysis:** Many nondepartmental members spend large amounts of time analyzing data, looking for trends, and using the information to better assess what course of action or next steps need to happen. For example, special educators regularly give assessments that they have to analyze for student response. They need to extrapolate this information so they can create an IEP to guarantee student learning. Academic counselors sift through and review course selection data to identify trends in educational preference that will help create the master schedule.

3. **Whole-child focus:** Because the school doesn't charge nondepartmental members with delivering specific content-area curriculum, they are able to focus on the whole child and not just academics. This focus enables them to use a different lens, which is critical, especially when we talk about student learning because so much learning depends on not only academic readiness but also where the learner is socially and emotionally.

4. **Skilled collaboration:** Due to the nature of the job, nondepartmental members spend a fair amount of time working with both students and adults. The time they spend with other professionals typically centers on four areas: (a) best practice, (b) latest research, (c) observational analysis,

and (d) consultation. These four areas can enhance collaboration as they help bring clarity and precision to any dialogue.

5. **Understanding of protocols:** Most nondepartmental members have developed, and follow, specific protocols that ensure safety, efficiency, and efficacy for their clients.

Nondepartmental members are one of the most underutilized groups in the school system when it comes to student learning. They are often overlooked simply because they don't have a subject-matter or content-area expertise. The fact is that most nondepartmental members talk with students all day long (as well as the adults in the building), so they receive large amounts of anecdotal information regarding students and their learning process. They also gather information about the adults and their struggles with helping students learn. This makes nondepartmental members a wealth of information that can truly help teachers perfect their craft. It is true that they receive much of this information in confidence and so they need to handle sharing delicately, but it is also true nondepartmental members can give feedback, whether general or specific, without breaking the confidence of the source.

While not in the classroom daily, nondepartmental members work directly with students who are. Students typically share anecdotal information about what's happening in their lives, and more specifically, what is going on in their education world. Some of this information may center on teachers, their learning strategies, the latest test or exam, or their thoughts or opinions on how a teacher may have done with a particular lesson plan that day. While this type of sharing might help alleviate some of the issues and concerns students face, it is also useful information nondepartmental members can share with teachers.

Teachers might say, "I really knocked it out of the park today," "I was on fire today," or "I could see the lightbulbs going off." Nondepartmental members, because of the nature of their jobs, often hear the other point of view to many of those comments, such as, "The teacher really droned on today," "We did the dumbest activities," or "The teacher was moving too fast, and it was hard to keep up." This dichotomy often shows the disconnect between teaching and learning. It also demonstrates how important it is for both sides to give and receive feedback regarding instruction. In most traditional schools, there is no structure for this type of feedback loop between the teacher and the student, and most of the time, that information goes to a nondepartmental member.

Besides anecdotal feedback regarding teaching and learning, much of the information nondepartmental members receive has to do with social-emotional concerns, struggles, past traumas, future concerns, or worries. These are all important pieces of the puzzle, particularly when we talk about student learning. Sometimes they are able to provide a more complete picture of a student's mental health and well-being in addition to academic progress. For example, perhaps the student just lost a parent, his or her parents are going through a divorce, or the student just ended a relationship. While this information may not necessarily help teachers with lesson planning or content delivery, it allows for more accurate and deeper understanding of the students in their class.

How Can Schools Effectively Place Nondepartmental Members on Established Teams?

Collaborative teams take time to develop, even within their own departments. Placing other members into a departmental team requires some background knowledge and dialogue with others to ensure team success. The worksheet in figure 7.1 can help clarify what each person has to offer a team.

How and Where Can Nondepartmental Members Impact Student and Adult Learning?

When building a team, team members must consider what area nondepartmental members might impact or contribute to. Nondepartmental members can not only assist with the following areas but also be valued and contributing members. These four areas include (1) classroom teaching, (2) curriculum development and lesson planning, (3) assessment and data analysis, and (4) tiered intervention.

Classroom Teaching

Creating the structure for a coteaching model can be relatively simple. However, changing the culture to embrace this model can be very difficult. Having two dedicated professionals inside the classroom working together to ensure student learning is an incredibly powerful model. When the two teachers can work in conjunction with each other, as opposed to two independents sharing the same space, amazing things happen for both the students and the teachers. This needs to be an intentional, collective commitment between both parties that administration supports to guarantee success. These professionals must strive to work through the awkward phase of establishing and clearly defining the *why* behind the work they need to

Nondepartmental Member Placement Worksheet

Nondepartmental member name: _____

Academic undergraduate and graduate background:

(for example, biology, history, Spanish)

_____

_____

_____

Established departmental relationships:

(for example, English 9, algebra 1,
auto shop or personal)

_____

_____

_____

Experience with data analysis (circle the appropriate number on the scale):

Little --- A lot
       1   2   3   4   5   6   7   8   9   10

Experience with curriculum development:

Little --- A lot
       1   2   3   4   5   6   7   8   9   10

Experience with RTI:

Little --- A lot
       1   2   3   4   5   6   7   8   9   10

Top-three choices for placement:

_____

_____

_____

Figure 7.1: Nondepartmental member placement worksheet.

*Visit **go.SolutionTree.com/PLCbooks** for a free reproducible version of this figure.*

accomplish. At the beginning of this relationship, both teachers might feel put upon, as each may see the other as a burden or hindrance to what he or she could accomplish alone.

While many would agree that having another set of eyes and ears inside the classroom can be incredibly productive for the learning process, in reality, it can also be daunting, as it may feel like another professional is evaluating your every move. Get together and intentionally talk about the purpose for having a coteaching model and how effective it can be to ensure that all students learn at high levels.

Collaboration between all team members should focus on learning. We often refer to this as engaging in true collaboration, not *coblaboration*, a term first coined by David Perkins (2003). This term suggests that team collaboration should move away from dress codes, tardy policies, field trips, parties, and so on, to a focus on answering important questions like, How do we know if our students are learning the essential standards? and What should we do when they are not learning and when they already know it? Move away from discussion with no action to more action and less talk.

Table 7.1 outlines five ways teams can move from coblaboration to collaboration. When team members keep the focus on student learning, students benefit.

Table 7.1: Moving From Coblaboration to Collaboration

Coblaboration	Collaboration
Focus on assigning blame or taking credit.	Focus on outcomes.
Stakeholders participate to protect.	Stakeholders participate to generate value.
Opinions rule.	Data are king.
Talk exceeds action.	Actions emerge from engagement.
This is an informal process.	This is an intentional, rigorous process.

Source: Thompson, 2013.

There are three different ways of being in an effective, collaborative relationship: (1) coordinate, (2) cooperate, and (3) collaborate. In most traditional schools, non-departmental members and general education teachers either cooperate or coordinate with each other in a coteaching scenario, making the learning for both teacher and student difficult. The goal is to truly *collaborate* with one another, ensuring that students learn at high levels. In order to develop this model to its full potential, teachers must set aside time to dissect curriculum, plan lessons, analyze data, create extension activities, and talk about tiered intervention.

Curriculum Development and Lesson Planning

When it comes to curriculum development and lesson planning, some nondepartmental members are highly trained in a variety of skills that can help struggling students connect to their learning. Their advanced training helps them identify learning challenges and devise a plan to help overcome them.

While general education teachers should typically have mastery over a particular content area, they are not always experts on how students with or without learning challenges may receive the information. For this reason, it is of utmost importance that they collaborate with others to help the curriculum design meet the needs of all students. This collaborative design leads to what Buffum et al. (2012) refer to as a more effective Tier 1 intervention, meaning more students will have access to their learning. This leads to better-quality delivery of Tier 2, Tier 3, and extensions.

Assessment and Data Analysis

Many traditional schools would rarely consider using someone outside the department for assessment development, whether the assessments be summative or formative. Because of their background, many nondepartmental members have had a great deal of exposure to and practice with test questions and protocols. This consistent practice allows them to quickly identify trends and patterns of students with learning challenges. The experience with data analysis makes nondepartmental members well versed in what a good assessment looks like and how to extrapolate data from the responses. When you couple this with nondepartmental members' background knowledge (for example, English, mathematics, science, and so on), you wind up with an expert who can help make the assessment development and data analysis processes clear and concise.

Most general education teachers have not had the same exposure to generating test questions or extrapolating data as the nondepartmental member. Therefore, it becomes a natural fit for the two to work together when creating these assessments. While the general education teacher may have more practical experience with specific content, nondepartmental members can ask the necessary questions to generate assessments that are truly going to gather specific information.

When departments or teams meet to discuss assessments or data analysis, most nondepartmental members can quickly and accurately assess student learning issues.

Because of their specific training, they are able to see patterns, which can lead to a deeper discussion around student learning. Data analysis becomes a key feature of the collaborative process.

Tiered Intervention

When it comes to tiered intervention in the RTI process, every school wants all students learning at high levels (grade level or better). Tier 1 represents what all students receive via core instruction. While each student is unique and has different learning issues, the initial core instruction should attempt to reach *all* students the first time. Schools use a tiered system of interventions because they realize that all students are unique, which means their learning is also unique. In other words, some students may not receive the intended instruction in a way that works for them. We also know that not all teachers, no matter how good they are, have all the necessary background, knowledge, and experience to help every student successfully navigate all content.

Working in collaborative teacher teams that include nondepartmental members is paramount to helping increase the opportunity for student success. Differentiation is the key to ensuring that more students learn the material at the Tier 1 level. Tiered intervention hinges on the idea of collective responsibility, meaning that teachers are responsible collectively, not only to each other but also to the students they serve. That collective responsibility, particularly as we move through the different tiers, is critical.

In joining forces and collaborating as teams, we will continue to see the most success from Tier 1. To make this successful, we need to commit to partnering nondepartmental members and general education teachers for classroom instruction, curricular design, data analysis, and tiered intervention.

Moving into a Tier 2 or Tier 3 support system requires a much more systematic and systemic approach to learning. While the general education teacher is still considered the content master, forming collaborative partnerships with nondepartmental members becomes paramount in Tier 2 and Tier 3 intervention. Tier 2 and Tier 3 require interventions in a specific curricular or content area that students have not mastered. For these tiers to be effective, teams must collaborate to isolate what the specific issue is and come up with a plan of attack for ensuring that students get the instruction they need to master that particular learning target or skill. This can only happen when the teams include nondepartmental members who can bring another level of understanding and intervention to the whole team.

Lastly, the advantage to having nondepartmental members in department meetings is that when teachers struggle with generating ideas for intervention, particularly at the Tier 1 and Tier 2 levels, nondepartmental members are a great resource. They can often help lead the team into a deeper-level discussion of how to use interventions to more effectively achieve the desired outcome, which is learning for all.

How Do We Ensure All Team Members Welcome and Accept Nondepartmental Members?

Collaboration can be difficult within your own department, so it is understandable that creating teams including nondepartmental members could be even more challenging. Creating effective collaborative teams requires intentionality and clarity so all parties understand the benefits (again, we'll invoke Schmoker's [2004] directive that clarity precedes competence). We should not throw individuals together or tell them to go forth and collaborate without some kind of direction. Being intentional about gathering background information as well as willing to nurture groups means a much better chance at developing successful teams that comprise a variety of professionals.

Forming new teams, like those including nondepartmental members, can be challenging. Because nondepartmental members often join teams that are already formed and working together, understanding the stages of team formation can be helpful. Bruce W. Tuckman (1965) offers the following four stages of team development: (1) forming, (2) storming, (3) norming, and (4) performing.

1. **Forming:** In this initial stage, team members exhibit polite behaviors, feeling out their roles and testing their relationships with each other. There is often excitement, anticipation, and anxiety around doing collaborative work.

2. **Storming:** During this stage, conflicts might emerge within the team, especially around interpersonal issues. There may be a clash over control of the group and its work. As teams storm, it is not unusual for passive-aggressive behaviors to emerge and for some to attempt to sabotage the group's work. Team members might become defensive or competitive, and some may even choose sides. Team members may establish unrealistic goals or workloads and end up frustrated at how little they accomplish.

3. **Norming:** In the norming stage, teams begin to work together more productively, and a positive team identity emerges. Members see the value of collaboration, and they have positive conversations. New leaders may emerge, and meetings are more likely to focus on achieving consensus. Teams make effective use of formal roles and rules to maintain harmony.

4. **Performing:** At this point, there is a high level of function. The team has developed strong interpersonal relationships, and there is a sense of attachment to the team. These relationships form out of trust and allow team members to disagree in constructive ways. The team internalizes the reflective processes and focuses on continuous improvement.

The early phases of forming collaborative teams that include nondepartmental members can be quite difficult. Unless a relationship has already been established, neither the nondepartmental members nor the departmental members may know their roles, their responsibilities, or how they should interact with each other. This awkwardness provides a great way to start a rich dialogue around the *why* of working collaboratively.

How to Coach Your Team

Your situation may not be identical to the scenario at the beginning of the chapter, but many schools share similar problems when adding team members who might not be an exact fit within the group. When adding additional team members, there are no shortcuts or easy ways to place new people on teams, especially when it feels like those people may not be a natural fit with the established team. Following are eight coaching tips to help make this transition successful and, in turn, increase the learning for both adults and students.

1. **Change the mindset:** The mindset of *we don't need this person* or *this person doesn't fit or make sense here* needs to change in order for teams to be successful. This is known as a *fixed mindset.* Carol Dweck (2016) states that when people have a fixed mindset, they believe basic qualities, like intelligence or talent, are fixed traits. When people have a growth mindset, they believe that basic abilities are developed through dedication and hard work. People with a growth mindset look at the possibilities and the advantages to having nondepartmental members as part of the team to enhance learning and productivity. It is often a good

idea for team members to list all the possibilities and advantages to having nondepartmental members as part of their team. This can help members reframe their view of the new people joining the team.

2. **Welcome new team members:** Figuring out how to welcome new people onto a team is of paramount importance. The team must decide how to welcome and incorporate new members into the team meetings so they feel like welcome and productive members. Remember, real change is real hard. Planning the details around the change will help mitigate some of the hurdles.

3. **Create clarity around the *why*:** The team needs to clearly establish the why of having new team members. Additionally, teams should not ignore the challenge they face in adapting to new members. Instead, team members should address this challenge and reach agreement on how new members will help them advance student learning.

4. **Address confusion:** Sometimes confusion around why certain team members are present can mimic negative attitudes or even hostile or aggressive behavior. Addressing the confusion by providing clarity can minimize the seemingly negative or hostile behavior and move the team toward higher performance.

5. **Facilitate the change:** The early phases of meeting as a collaborative team that includes nondepartmental members might be awkward. This challenge is a great way to start a rich dialogue around working collaboratively. You may want someone outside the team, such as a school leader, to facilitate this initial conversation. Once you achieve clarity, make commitments, and establish norms, you can begin the work in earnest.

6. **Practice, practice, practice:** The only way to get better at something is to practice. Forming a new team is no different. At first, it will be clunky and awkward, and may not bring out the best behaviors you want in a team. As you continue to nurture each other's strengths and commit to focusing on student learning, that awkwardness fades away and is replaced by productive, healthy learning dialogues.

7. **Make it safe to disagree:** Team members do not always need to be like minded, but they do need to agree on outcomes. Disagreement is not always about right or wrong; it is a process of examining

differing viewpoints. Create an atmosphere in which the team can ask honest questions and express genuine concern that allows for a healthy discussion.

8. **Establish core values:** Much like norms, teams need to establish core values. Values provide an anchor. Team values will create clarity and help guide learning outcomes.

Conclusion

The bottom line is that creating teams that consist of departmental and non-departmental personnel can be daunting, but schools can reap huge rewards when it comes to student and adult learning. Having nondepartmental members attend department meetings, subject-level team meetings, content team meetings, or grade-level meetings at least monthly can be very powerful, particularly as they review information in light of best practice. Because of the information they receive, it may be helpful that they engage with your teams to enhance learning for all.

Additional Resources

Teams can use these helpful resources to gain further guidance and insights for their collaborative work.

- *Learning by Doing: A Handbook for Professional Learning Communities at Work* **(3rd ed.):** Most PLC experts would agree that *Learning by Doing* (DuFour et al., 2016) is the bible of PLC literature. Schools use this book when searching for research and practice into the art of helping all students learn at high levels. When it comes to education, knowledge, and research regarding collaborative teams, three specific chapters (chapters 3, 9, and 10) flesh out the details for understanding how to build a collaborative culture that focuses on teams, address conflicts that may result from moving to a collaborative culture, and move forward in the implementation process.

- *Concise Answers to Frequently Asked Questions About Professional Learning Communities at Work:* In chapter 2 of this 2016 publication, Mattos et al. talk specifically about how to foster a collaborative culture, what the criteria should be when forming a collaborative team, the optimal size for teacher teams, the pitfalls of forming teams, and the types of teams that schools should form.

- ***Simplifying Response to Intervention: Four Essential Guiding Principles***: In chapter 7 and the epilogue of this book, authors Buffum et al. (2012) emphasize how we get every student "there" (learning at high levels), regardless of designation, learning challenge, or ability. They also discuss how to move from general education or special education to education for all.

- ***Yes We Can! General and Special Educators Collaborating in a Professional Learning Community***: In this book, authors Heather Friziellie, Julie A. Schmidt, and Jeanne Spiller (2016) discuss how general and special educators can collaborate within a professional learning community, which in turn improves the outcome for all students. They review step-by-step strategies for establishing what all students should learn, designing standards, aligning instruction, creating assessments, monitoring progress, and responding when students don't learn.

Supporting Singleton Teachers in Collaborative Teams

When teachers examine the standards in isolation, each teacher is likely to interpret the intent and rigor of the standards differently. This results in a different level of student expectations and quality of instruction from class to class.

—Kim Bailey, Chris Jakicic, and Jeanne Spiller

The Story of Clayton Middle School

At Clayton Middle School, there is typically only one teacher per content area on a grade-level team, such as one mathematics teacher, one English teacher, one science teacher, and one social studies teacher. When meeting as grade-level teams, their conversations generally center on a few students having difficulty or causing problems in each of their classes. They usually finish their collaborative meetings feeling as if they have accomplished very little related to teaching or, more important, learning. They rarely discuss essential learning standards or their expectations related to the standards.

One teacher says, "I teach seventh-grade mathematics. It really doesn't help me to discuss my content with the other seventh-grade teachers because I'm the only one who teaches it. I don't see the point in meeting with them about mathematics. I see how discussing students is helpful but not specific subjects."

Wisely, the seventh-grade team leader begins to realize that all teachers really could benefit from meeting with their subject-specific colleagues to discuss the learning progression from sixth to eighth grade. She approaches the principal to see if there is time in the schedule when her seventh-grade team can meet with content-specific sixth-grade and eighth-grade teachers.

She communicates the desire for each of her teammates to have content-specific discussions with both the sixth-grade and eighth-grade teachers. She explains that they are excited to talk with the sixth-grade teachers about how they are preparing students for seventh grade and what standards they consider essential for all sixth graders to know and be able to do. They want to know the methods they are using to teach the standards, what is working well, and their expectations for mastery of the standards. She expresses her excitement about the chance to have discussions with the eighth-grade teachers about what they hope seventh graders will come to them knowing and being able to do as they enter eighth grade in each content area.

Principal Smart is thrilled that one of her grade-level team leaders is interested in collaborating with content-specific teachers. She has tried to communicate the value in the past to no avail. She immediately recognizes that it will be a challenge to make this happen but agrees to take a look at the master schedule to see if she can make it work.

Principal Smart decides the best way for content-specific teams to meet is to dedicate staff meeting time to this mixed-grade, content-alike collaboration. In fact, she dedicates forty-five minutes of every other sixty-minute staff meeting to this collaboration. Since staff meetings take place weekly, this allows vertical, content-specific teams to meet every other week for forty-five minutes.

Principal Smart first meets with the entire staff as a whole for fifteen minutes to review any important information she could not review via email, and then she disperses teams to their content-alike meetings. Principal Smart works with district staff to refocus early release days so they can provide another opportunity for singleton teachers to meet with others who teach the same subjects at different schools. She also assures teams that she will continue looking at ways she can adjust the master schedule to allow for more meaningful collaborative time.

As the teams become more comfortable working together and begin to see the benefits, team leaders guide mixed-grade, content-alike teams in the process of unpacking standards so they can come to clarity and agreement on essential standards per grade and by course. Now, when teacher teams meet, they discuss the skills students will need to demonstrate mastery of essential standards.

For example, English language arts teachers design common rubrics on argumentative writing that sixth-, seventh-, and eighth-grade classes can use. Mathematics teachers often stand together at the whiteboard showing each other how they teach specific concepts so there is consistency from one grade level to the next. The music teachers meet monthly with other music teachers from around the district to unpack standards and come to agreement on essential standards per course or grade level. Singleton middle school teachers, even though they each teach a separate course, now work collaboratively within content areas to improve student learning on essential standards.

The teachers at Clayton Middle School are similar to many singleton teachers at middle schools who meet as grade-level teams rather than content-area teams. This shift in practice is often difficult due to the mindset of always meeting as grade-level teams. They also wonder if meeting together as mathematics teachers will be as productive as they hoped. However, once these teams see the benefit of working together in content-area teams, they are excited for their weekly collaboration time. In this chapter, we offer strategies for how to include and support singleton teachers in collaborative teamwork.

What the Experts Say

Building a collaborative culture is one of the tenets of an effective PLC. It is imperative that all teachers have the opportunity to collaborate with others, even if they are the only ones in the school teaching a particular subject. According to DuFour (2003), all professionals in a school are obligated to seek and apply best practice. Best practice for improving professionals and meeting student needs is to build a collaborative culture.

Collaboration can be challenging for schools with singleton teachers, but nonetheless, we must find a way to make it happen in a meaningful and productive way. If we simply find ways for singletons to collaborate by adjusting the master schedule or by using time differently, we fail to focus on what they are collaborating about;

and it is unlikely that the collaboration will have a positive impact on student achievement. Saunders, Goldenberg, and Gallimore (2009) conclude:

> A common feature of PLCs that reported achievement gains was teacher teams focusing on improving instruction and achievement. Time for collaboration by itself, even when administratively supported, is unlikely to improve [student] achievement unless additional conditions are in place that structure its use. (p. 1028)

The structure that Vicki Vescio and her colleagues (2008) refer to means that the focus of collaboration is teaching and learning. Robert Miller and Brian Rowan (2006) further substantiate this finding, indicating that a lack of focus on curriculum and instruction during teacher meetings could possibly explain the absence of a relationship between student achievement and teacher reports of staff collaboration, teacher empowerment, and supportive administration. According to Aaron Hansen (2015), author of *How to Develop PLCs for Singletons and Small Schools*, a high-functioning team shares strategies, models lessons for each other, and learns and tries new strategies together. Teachers improve their professional practice in practical ways by using their own student data as a means for collaboratively improving what they do.

The ideas and practices we address in the following common questions provide examples of the structures and protocols singleton teachers can engage in to ensure that they focus collaboration on actions to improve student achievement.

Common Questions About Singletons in Collaborative Teams

Following are the answers to common questions teams might ask about involving singleton teachers in your collaborative teams, including the challenges and benefits of this collaboration.

Chapter 1 of this book (page 5) discusses the six types of collaborative teams. Schools can use these same team structures, with modification, to provide collaborative opportunities for singleton teachers.

1. Horizontal teams

2. Vertical teams

3. Logical links

4. Interdisciplinary teams

5. District or regional teams

6. Digital teams

How Do Horizontal Teams Support Singletons?

These teams consist of teachers who teach the same course or grade level. This structure is common in larger schools where multiple teachers teach the same grade or the same course. For example, there are four sophomore English teachers or three fifth-grade teachers. This makes it convenient to collaborate since everyone is teaching the exact same class.

The five-step process for horizontal teams to establish a guaranteed and viable curriculum is as follows.

1. Unpack the standards as a team for clarity and agreement.

2. Identify the essential or priority standards for the grade level or course.

3. Map out units of study based on essential standards.

4. As a team, create assessments around the essential standards for each unit of study.

5. Collaboratively analyze common formative assessment data to determine skill-specific interventions and extensions for students.

Consider a word of caution to teachers on horizontal teams. Some teachers turn themselves into singletons by choosing to departmentalize on a grade level or by having one teacher take all the grade-specific students at the secondary level. For example, Mr. Hernandez has three sections of sixth-grade English language arts, Mrs. Cruz has three sections of seventh-grade English language arts, and Ms. Allen has three sections of eighth-grade English language arts. In order to work on a horizontal team, Mr. Hernandez would teach two sixth-grade sections and one seventh-grade section, Mrs. Cruz would teach one sixth-grade section and two eighth-grade sections, and Ms. Allen would teach two seventh-grade sections and one eighth-grade section. See figure 8.1.

Teacher	Grade 6	Grade 7	Grade 8
Hernandez	Two sections	One section	
Cruz	One section		Two sections
Allen		Two sections	One section

Figure 8.1: Horizontal team for English language arts.

With this structure in place, all three teachers now have another teacher who teaches the same course. They are now able to collaboratively design grade-specific lessons around essential standards, design common assessments, analyze data, and provide interventions and extensions to meet the needs of their students.

How Do Vertical Teams Support Singletons?

These teams consist of teachers who teach the same content across different grade levels (for example, a language arts team that includes a kindergarten teacher, a first-grade teacher, and a second-grade teacher). This structure is especially useful for small schools that often only have one teacher per subject.

The five-step process for vertical teams to establish a guaranteed and viable curriculum is as follows.

1. Unpack the standards as a team.

2. Identify the essential or priority standards for each grade level.

3. Map out a unit of study based on two to three essential standards, and modify it for each grade level.

4. As a team, create assessments around the essential standards for each grade level.

5. Share strategies to teach essential standards.

Consider the essential standard example in figure 8.2. See how the Common Core standard CCRA.R.1 (NGA & CCSSO, 2010) evolves from kindergarten through grade 12. If you are a singleton teacher in sixth, seventh, or eighth grade, your standards are almost identical to those of singletons in the other two grades.

Teachers on this vertical team unpack the standard, determine depth of knowledge and academic vocabulary, and list examples of how to teach and assess the standard. The team then collaboratively determines what it would look like for a student in sixth grade, seventh grade, and eighth grade to master the standard. Teachers then share artifacts to show the continuum of learning from one grade level to the next.

Teachers in a department may also collaboratively design courses based on essential standards. Consider this example: Todd, Jenn, and Dallas meet to design a guaranteed and viable curriculum for integrated mathematics 1, 2, and 3. They collaboratively design these classes as a team rather than viewing them as classes

College and Career Anchor Standard for Reading (Key Ideas and Details)			
1. Read closely to determine what the text says explicitly and to make logical inferences from it. Cite specific textual evidence when writing or speaking to support conclusions drawn from the text.			
Reading Standard for Literature			
Kindergarten	**Grade 1**	**Grade 2**	**Grade 3**
With prompting and support, ask and answer questions about key details in a text.	Ask and answer questions about key details in a text.	Ask and answer such questions as who, what, where, when, why, and how to demonstrate understanding of key details in a text.	Ask and answer questions to demonstrate understanding of a text, referring explicitly to the text as the basis for the answers.
Grade 4	**Grade 5**	**Grade 6**	**Grade 7**
Refer to details and examples in a text when explaining what the text says explicitly and when drawing inferences from the text.	Quote accurately from a text when explaining what the text says explicitly and when drawing inferences from the text.	Cite textual evidence to support analysis of what the text says explicitly as well as inferences drawn from the text.	Cite several pieces of textual evidence to support analysis of what the text says explicitly as well as inferences drawn from the text.
Grade 8	**Grades 9–10**	**Grades 11–12**	
Cite the textual evidence that most strongly supports an analysis of what the text says explicitly as well as inferences drawn from the text.	Cite strong and thorough textual evidence to support analysis of what the text says explicitly as well as inferences drawn from the text.	Cite strong and thorough textual evidence to support analysis of what the text says explicitly as well as inferences drawn from the text, including determining when the text leaves matters uncertain.	

Source for standards: NGA & CCSSO, 2010.

Figure 8.2: Example of CCSS.ELA-Literacy.CCRA.R.1 across grade levels.

belonging to a particular teacher. This process ensures student mastery of essential standards in a systematic flow from one course to the next.

They follow this three-step process.

1. Unpack the standards for each course.

2. Identify essential standards per course.

3. Pace standards for the school year.

How Do Logical Links Support Singletons?

These teams consist of teachers who are pursuing the same learning outcomes. Teachers in special education or specialist subjects, such as music, art, and career and technical education, choose a set of essential standards to use in all their classes.

Logical links teams use the following four-step process.

1. Identify a common essential standard.

2. Unpack the standard for clarity and agree on what it looks like for students to master the standard.

3. Model teaching the standard for each other.

4. Write a common assessment to measure student mastery of the essential standard.

An example of logical links would be teachers using a common rubric on an argumentative essay across all music, art, and career and technical education classes, citing textual evidence or reading and comprehending on grade level. The content may be different in each class, but the learning target on the essential standard would be the same. The welding teacher may ask students to argue the benefits of using the MIG welder over the stick welder, while the art teacher may ask students to argue the most influential artist of the baroque period.

How Do Interdisciplinary Teams Support Singletons?

Interdisciplinary teams consist of teachers who share common outcomes across different content. In one high school, where all teachers are singletons, the teachers plan a thematic unit of study around carefully selected essential standards. While discussing these common standards, the teams decided to use the book *The Immortal Life of Henrietta Lacks* by Rebecca Skloot (2011) as a common theme. Henrietta Lacks was an African American woman whose cancer cells have been used in research around the world. English language arts classes read *Henrietta Lacks*, while the science class explores cell formation. While this is happening, the social studies teacher is discussing the civil rights movement and what was happening in the United States in the early 1950s.

The important part of the process is that team members collaborate more deeply around the standards than merely using the same theme. Following are the three steps in their collaborative process.

1. Identify a common essential standard for all three courses, such as main idea and key details in a text.

2. Identify additional essential standards for each content area.

3. Backward-design all assessments per content area as a collaborative team.

This process starts with the final unit assessment and then breaks the unit assessment into smaller common formative assessments throughout the unit of study. Teacher teams not only design each assessment together, but also take the assessments together to determine tricky questions they might need to change. They also discuss how to administer, score, and determine proficiency for the assessments.

Next, they map out what should be happening in each course on a daily basis. They place assessments appropriately throughout the unit of study by course.

When they administer an assessment in a particular course, all teachers look at the data together to discuss the following.

- What worked well?

- Where do our students struggle the most?

- Which items did they most frequently miss and why?

- How can we improve the assessment?

- What teaching strategies can we share?

- What is our plan of action for skill-specific intervention and extension?

- What students need additional interventions or extensions?

How Do District or Regional Teams Support Singletons?

District or regional teams consist of teachers who want to align outcomes across an entire district or region (for example, the district's secondary band teachers).

District teams comprise teachers from around the district who teach the same course or grade level.

Consider these five steps as a district grade level or course.

1. Identify a SMART goal for the team.

2. Identify essential standards.

3. Create a pacing guide for your grade-level subject or course.

4. Write common assessments.

5. Meet monthly to analyze common assessment data.

Note the following example. Kindergarten teachers from one district meet at the district office. Their year-long goal is to unpack standards, identify essential or priority standards, and write common assessments as a collaborative team. There are over two dozen teachers in the room using their collective strengths and expertise to determine a guaranteed and viable curriculum for all students districtwide.

After their initial meeting, teachers meet monthly at the district office or at a host school in the district. During this time, they share best practices and strategies around essential standards and look at data from common assessments to improve student and adult learning. It is a win for teachers and student learning.

How Do Digital Teams Support Singletons?

Digital teams consist of teachers who seek connections with colleagues across the district, state, or world. This team structure is especially useful for singleton teachers who are the only ones to teach a subject, such as art, music, welding, or drama, in their schools.

Consider these five steps for digital teams.

1. Unpack the standards together to provide clarity and agreement on what it looks like to teach and assess the standards.

2. Identify the essential or priority standards.

3. Map out units of study based on two to three essential standards.

4. Create common assessments or rubrics around the essential standards.

5. Analyze common assessments together to improve student and adult learning.

Note the following example. Susan, an art teacher in Alabama, is having a difficult time finding someone to collaborate with in her small district. Dan, an art teacher from Idaho, is having a difficult time finding someone to collaborate with in his small town. They become friends on a social media site for art teachers. Despite hailing from different states and time zones, they become a collaborative team, planning lessons around essential standards, writing common rubrics, taking pictures of art projects and sending them back and forth, and improving their student learning outcomes and skills as teachers. They function as a thriving team.

How to Coach Your Team

Coaching a singleton requires thinking outside the box. Singletons have unique challenges regarding collaboration that may require creative thinking and flexibility. Here are seven tips to consider.

1. As with all teams, coach singletons on *why* they are collaborating together. Often singletons picture themselves working in isolation as the only art teacher or welding teacher. Some singletons even enjoy the fact that they don't have someone else to worry about. It will, therefore, be critical to coach singletons through the value of working with other teachers who teach the same content area. What are the benefits of working together to gain clarity on essential standards? What does it look like for students to master the standards?

2. Once singleton teachers understand why they should collaborate, they need to understand how they should collaborate. As we discussed previously in this chapter, this may require driving to another school or using technology to connect.

3. Singleton teachers often feel isolated or disconnected with the school's collective team collaborative process. It is, therefore, important to help singleton teachers see the broader schoolwide goals and find meaningful ways to contribute. But this perspective is often limited to the singleton teacher looking for a team within the school rather than focusing on broad school goals such as reading and comprehending on grade level.

4. Encourage singletons to look beyond the walls of their school for those who teach courses with the same content and standards. Generally speaking, you can find other teachers within a district who share content. Singletons can reach outside their schools and even their

districts to find teachers in surrounding areas to collaborate with around essential standards.

5. Singletons can use digital tools, such as Google Hangouts, Skype, and Zoom, to provide the digital means to meet with team members who are not in the same location.

6. Once you identify singletons and they form teams, it is important to the teams' success to establish SMART goals for which team members are mutually accountable. SMART goals may include giving curricular priority to essential standards, developing common formative assessments for each essential standard, reviewing data, and increasing proficiency on district benchmark assessments and state end-of-level tests.

7. The main benefit of collaboration for a singleton is increased student achievement and teaching capacity.

Conclusion

There are many ways for singleton teachers to collaborate as a PLC. It requires creative thinking, planning, and scheduling. This chapter provided six structures that support singletons and help them become part of collaborative efforts: (1) horizontal teams, (2) vertical teams, (3) logical links, (4) interdisciplinary teams, (5) district or regional teams, and (6) digital teams. All these team structures can benefit from singletons being part of the process. Singletons can bring unique and valuable perspectives to teams across schools and districts.

Additional Resources

Teams can use these helpful resources to gain further guidance and insights for their collaborative work.

*   ***It's About Time: Planning Interventions and Extensions in Elementary School:*** This 2014 publication edited by Austin Buffum and Mike Mattos addresses how elementary schools can impact student learning by developing a guaranteed and viable curriculum, common assessments that measure student proficiency of essential standards, and intervention systems that provide the time and support students

need to be successful. All collaborative teams can benefit from the ideas discussed in this thought-provoking book full of practical strategies.

- *It's About Time: Planning Interventions and Extensions in Secondary School*: Mike Mattos and Austin Buffum (2014) address how to find time in the school day for effective intervention in schools. The text includes strategies for scheduling as well as ideas for how to provide intervention that makes a difference for students. Examples of schools that have been successful implementing strong intervention systems provide ideas for teams to consider as they develop their intervention systems.

- *How to Develop PLCs for Singletons and Small Schools*: In this helpful resource, Aaron Hansen (2015) describes five different ways schools can organize teams to help singletons and small schools participate fully in the PLC process. These five strategies help teachers and other staff members more fully integrate with each other to form high-functioning teams.

Epilogue:
Dealing With Cautions,
Conflicts, and Commitments

Individual commitment to a group effort—that is what makes a
team work, a company work, a society work, a civilization work.

—Vince Lombardi

Creating effective collaborative teams is far more complex than it might appear at first glance. As educators, it is imperative that we work through these challenges. At the heart of this book is a shared desire to help your team better ensure that every student you serve learns at high levels and is prepared for the next unit, the next grade level, and beyond. As we conclude, we want to share a few final thoughts, or what we refer to as cautions, conflicts, and commitments.

Cautions

As teams begin this critical work, it is important to pay close attention to different team dynamics that can affect a team's work. In order to help your team, we have identified characteristics of teams that may appear to be highly collaborative and effective, but in reality may function as just a group of individuals who come together occasionally to discuss students.

The Congenial Team Versus Your Collaborative Team

Following is a description of what we call the *congenial team*. After reading this description, compare it to your own collaborative team.

The Congenial Team

The fourth-grade team is the envy of all staff at Weiss Elementary School. Team members are competent, kindhearted educators and great people. The four team-mates are congenial colleagues and fast friends. They are similar in age and grew up in the same part of the country. They eat lunch together daily, post pictures of their weekend outings on social media, and generally spend a lot of time together. They are revered as a shining example of a high-functioning collaborative team. There is one problem: the student data over several years indicate that students are not making adequate progress.

Your Collaborative Team

What is the status of your collaborative team? Is your team more congenial than truly collaborative? Do you maintain an equal balance of both collegiality (the respectful relationship between those who work together in a similar capacity) and congeniality (the degree to which people get along)? Are you focused on the *right work*, as we have discussed throughout the book? Are your students growing and demonstrating their mastery of learning expectations? Let's make a clear distinction; when we think about successful teams in education, we must measure success by their impact on student learning.

The Tasky Team Versus Your Collaborative Team

Following is a description of what we call the *tasky team*. After reading this description, compare it to your own collaborative team.

The Tasky Team

The second-grade team at Smiley Elementary School is another team that many admire. It is typically the first team to complete its morning attendance and the first to finish its report cards, and the members never seem fazed by new initiatives or expectations. When the school asks this team to complete a task, it figures out the quickest way to accomplish it, often deciding to divide and conquer the work. Team members even share lesson planning, dividing up the lessons in a unit so they can get through the process faster. Their goal is efficiency over everything else, including collaboration. They rarely discuss student learning or common expectations for student proficiency. To them, this type of collaboration is inefficient and unnecessary. They do not see the value in discussion, reflection, and collective thinking and planning. As a result, the second graders show little growth from fall to winter and even lower growth from winter to spring.

Your Collaborative Team

How does your team approach tasks? Do you engage in conversations that are thoughtful, purposeful, and focused on students? Do you approach tasks collectively, or do you work in isolation in the name of efficiency? High-functioning collaborative teams recognize that the best way for them to focus on their goal of high levels of learning for all students is to work together. They create opportunities to collaborate as much as possible and reject the idea that *done is good*. They embrace professional discussion and conflict, recognizing that they can learn from different perspectives and opinions.

Think about the type of team you are currently working on. Is your team congenial or collaborative? What do your team agendas look like? Examine the agendas for a few weeks to determine patterns. Is there a focus on student learning, or do tasks consist of mostly informational items? What needs to shift so all your students meet grade-level expectations? We ask you to be honest about your current status and caution you not to be fooled by congeniality and efficiency as traits of high-functioning collaborative teams.

Conflicts

Simon and Garfunkel. The 1977 New York Yankees. Dean Martin and Jerry Lewis. What do these famous teams have in common? They were all highly successful, and all rose to the top of their respective fields. But all these teams also have something else in common. Despite their undeniable success, these famous teams didn't always get along. As with any successful team, your team will experience differences of opinion and conflict. It is important to note that conflict can generally be grouped into two categories: (1) healthy and (2) unhealthy. We're not suggesting that constant conflict is a necessary characteristic for a successful team. We are, however, confident that there is a time and place for engaging in healthy, productive conflict that challenges thinking and moves a team forward.

A common misperception is that high-functioning teams are conflict-free. In reality, successful collaborative teams don't avoid conflict; they embrace it. Strong teams are able to engage in lively debate without it eroding trust or compromising their ability to get their work done. Teams consist of people, and people aren't perfect. They come with different personalities and perspectives, which can occasionally lead to conflict. In order to be highly effective, collaborative teams must welcome healthy conflict and see it as a natural and necessary part of growing. According to Tom Rath and Barry Conchie (2008):

> Conflict doesn't destroy strong teams because strong teams focus on results. Contrary to popular belief, the most successful teams are not the ones in which team members always agree with one another. Instead, they are often characterized by healthy debate—and at times, heated arguments. What distinguishes strong teams from dysfunctional ones is that debate doesn't cause them to fragment. (pp. 71–72)

When considering conflict, author Daniel Levi (2011) clearly defines a difference between healthy and unhealthy conflict that teams experience (see table E.1).

Table E.1: Healthy Conflict Versus Unhealthy Conflict

Healthy	Unhealthy
• Focus on task issues • Legitimate differences of opinion about the task • Differences in values and perspectives • Different expectations about the impact of decisions	• Competition over power, rewards, and resources • Conflict between individual and group goals • Poorly run team meetings • Personal grudges from the past • Faulty communication

Source: Levi, 2011.

The majority of conflict that occurs on school teams falls into the *healthy* category—conflict rooted in ideas and values. Occasionally, teams dealing with *unhealthy* conflict may need a facilitator, a mediator, or more direct intervention from an administrator to get refocused on the correct work. Unfortunately, many teams have the preconceived notion that *any* conflict is bad, often for no other reason than it doesn't feel natural or comfortable. For some, moments of discomfort are negative and impact future efforts to collaborate. So how can we more effectively manage conflict on a collaborative team? Consider the following four strategies offered by Michael Bayewitz (2015):

1. Establish a Q-TIP rule (quit taking it personally). Remember, your primary purpose is to ensure student learning. When students don't learn the first time, don't take it personally. When a teammate has had more fruitful success with her students, don't take it personally. Model a spirit of inquiry with your teammates about what has worked best for them and share your collective successes.

2. Invite healthy conflict. Create regular meeting norms for your team and review them at the beginning of each meeting. This will help create the conditions to engage in healthy, honest exchanges that are designed to create better outcomes for students.

3. Monitor non-verbal communication. Research indicates that only 7% of what you communicate is through the words themselves (Mehrabian, 1981). Body language and gestures send powerful messages, as do the tone, rate of speech, and the volume of your voice. Pay attention to any and all non-verbal signals you may be giving.

4. Vary your approach. Is your teammate a veteran or a new teacher? Is it October or March? What have been your interactions with this colleague in the past? Consider these as well as other variables including personality, learning style, and life experience.

PLCs are characterized by having strong cultures, built on the pillars of having their shared mission, vision, values, and goals. Highly effective teams embrace student learning as their primary purpose yet occasionally must engage in difficult conversations in order to make this a reality. These kinds of conversations, though difficult and uncomfortable, are crucial. When teams establish trust and purpose, they have set the conditions for high levels of learning for both students and adults (Bayewitz, 2015).

Commitments

Collaborative teams that commit to doing the right work are the cog that drives the PLC engine. If we are to close the achievement gap so all students learn at high levels, it will take a committed, collective effort. If *all* means *all*, it is unreasonable to assume that one teacher can accomplish this in isolation. It takes the power of a committed team. While the work of teams is complex, we have the moral responsibility to implement what we know works in order to create the conditions for all students to learn at high levels. Truth be told, in the traditional system of schooling in the United States, we've been functioning in groups and not been working in highly effective teams. In traditional U.S. schools, this variance is not just the norm; it is accepted.

Keep in mind that effective collaboration takes *commitment* and *practice*. Consider a marching band during a football halftime show. You might see what appears to be a tightly planned sequence to produce a stunning visual and musical display for its audience. Upon seeing this kind of coordinated performance, it's easy to assume that creating it would take many hours of tedious practice. Obviously, a high-performing team like this would require practice, make frequent mistakes, and gain an abundance of learning. Each team member needs to learn his or her specific role on the field as well as the big picture for what the performance will look like as the individual parts work interdependently.

We can apply this same logic to the work of teams in a school. Does the team have a clear and compelling picture for what *highly effective* looks like? Does the team *practice*? Collaboration takes practice and certainly isn't successful on the first attempt. It takes time, repetition, and shared learning. Often, schools assemble teams and expect them to function without clear expectations. As a result, teams will attempt to collaborate, run into an issue, and quickly throw their arms in the air assuming their team is incapable of ever effectively working together. Future meetings are then sabotaged by the fact that some team members walk in with a sense of defeat with minimal engagement in the process. Educators often forget that to function as an effective team in any field requires repetition, practice, and learning from frequent mistakes. This shared learning is what defines a PLC.

If we are truly serious about closing the achievement gap, if we are truly serious that *all* means *all*, we cannot accept significant variance as the status quo. We must take total ownership of *all* students, and the only way we can do that is make a personal and professional commitment to them. How do we impact students whom we don't teach? We impact all students by functioning in highly effective teams and ensuring that their teachers have access to the most successful strategies and resources that lie in the collective expertise of the team. When we find excellence in practice, we seek to share and operationalize it.

Our final message to you is simple: make the commitment! Commit to ensuring that *every* student learns at high levels. Commit to working together in highly effective teams, and commit to collectively learning by doing. By definition, the PLC process is characterized by ongoing cycles of collective inquiry through job-embedded professional learning. This process is a journey of learning, characterized by practice and learning not only for students but also for the professionals who serve them. We truly are learning together.

References and Resources

Ainsworth, L. (2003). *Power standards: Identifying the standards that matter the most.* Englewood, CO: Advanced Learning Press.

Ainsworth, L. (2013). *Prioritizing the Common Core: Identifying specific standards to emphasize the most.* Englewood, CO: Lead + Learn Press.

Bailey, K., & Jakicic, C., (2011). *Common formative assessment: A toolkit for Professional Learning Communities at Work.* Bloomington, IN: Solution Tree Press.

Bailey, K., Jakicic, C. & Spiller, J. (2014). *Collaborating for success with the Common Core: A toolkit for Professional Learning Communities at Work.* Bloomington, IN: Solution Tree Press.

Barber, M., Chijioke, C., & Mourshed, M. (2010). *How the world's most improved school systems keep getting better.* Accessed at www.mckinsey.com/industries/social -sector/our-insights/how-the-worlds-most-improved-school-systems-keep-getting -better on February 24, 2017.

Barber, M., & Mourshed, M. (2007). *How the world's best-performing school systems come out on top.* Accessed at http://mckinseyonsociety.com/how-the-worlds-best -performing-schools-come-out-on-top on February 24, 2017.

Bayewitz, M. (2015, October 28). *Dealing with conflict on collaborative teams* [Blog post]. Accessed at www.allthingsplc.info/blog/view/315/Dealing+With+Conflict +on+Collaborative+Teams on June 23, 2019.

BrainyQuote. (n.d.). *Oscar Wilde.* Accessed at www.brainyquote.com/quotes/oscar _wilde_105029 on July 29, 2019.

Bryk, A., Gomez, L. M., Grunow, A., & LeMahieu, P. G. (2015). *Learning to improve: How America's schools can get better at getting better.* Cambridge, MA: Harvard Education Press.

Buffum, A., & Mattos, M. (Eds.). (2014). *It's about time: Planning interventions and extensions in elementary school.* Bloomington, IN: Solution Tree Press.

Buffum, A., Mattos, M., & Malone, J. (2018). *Taking action: A handbook for RTI at Work.* Bloomington, IN: Solution Tree Press.

Buffum, A., Mattos, M., & Weber, C. (2009). *Pyramid response to intervention: RTI, professional learning communities, and how to respond when kids don't learn.* Bloomington, IN: Solution Tree Press.

Buffum, A., Mattos, M., & Weber, C. (2012). *Simplifying response to intervention: Four essential guiding principles.* Bloomington, IN: Solution Tree Press.

Buffum, A., Mattos, M., Weber, C., & Hierck, T. (2015). *Uniting academic and behavior interventions: Solving the skill or will dilemma.* Bloomington, IN: Solution Tree Press.

Collins, J. (2001). *Good to great: Why some companies make the leap . . . and others don't.* New York: Harper Business.

Conley, R. (2015, September 25). *4 basic human needs leaders must meet to have engaged employees* [Blog post]. Accessed at https://leaderchat.org/2015/09/24/4 -basic-human-needs-leaders-must-meet-to-have-engaged-employees on September 26, 2018.

Deal, T. E., & Peterson, K. D. (1994). *The leadership paradox: Balancing logic and artistry in schools.* San Francisco: Jossey-Bass.

Deal, T. E., & Peterson, K. D. (1998). *Shaping school culture: The heart of leadership.* San Francisco: Jossey-Bass.

Donohoo, J. (2017). *Collective efficacy: How educators' beliefs impact student learning.* Thousand Oaks, CA: Corwin Press.

Donohoo, J., Hattie, J., & Eells, R. (2018). The power of collective efficacy. *Educational Leadership, 75*(6), 40–44.

Dubois, P. (1890). Reminiscences of President Garfield. *The Pennsylvania School Journal, 1*(39). Lancaster, PA: Inquirer Printing and Publishing Company. Accessed at https://books.google.com/books?id=AhtRAQAAMAAJ&printsec=frontcover &source=gbs_ge_summary_r&cad=0#v=onepage&q&f=false on June 20, 2019.

DuFour, R. (Director). (2002). *How to develop a professional learning community: Passion and persistence* [DVD]. Bloomington, IN: Solution Tree Press.

DuFour, R. (2003). Leading edge: "Collaboration lite" puts student achievement on a starvation diet. *Journal of Staff Development, 24*(3), 63–64.

DuFour, R., DuFour, R., & Eaker, R. (2008). *Revisiting Professional Learning Communities at Work: New insights for improving schools.* Bloomington, IN: Solution Tree Press.

DuFour, R., DuFour, R., Eaker, R., Many, T. W., & Mattos, M. (2016). *Learning by doing: A handbook for Professional Learning Communities at Work* (3rd ed.). Bloomington, IN: Solution Tree Press.

DuFour, R., & Eaker, R. (1998). *Professional Learning Communities at Work: Best practices for enhancing student achievement.* Bloomington, IN: Solution Tree Press.

DuFour, R., & Fullan, M. (2013). *Cultures built to last: Systemic PLCs at Work.* Bloomington, IN: Solution Tree Press.

DuFour, R., & Marzano, R. J. (2011). *Leaders of learning: How district, school, and classroom leaders improve student achievement.* Bloomington, IN: Solution Tree Press.

Dweck, C. S. (2016). *Mindset: The new psychology of success.* New York: Random House.

Elmore, R. F. (2002). Bridging the gap between standards and achievement: The imperative for professional development in education. *Albert Shanker Institute,* 44.

Elmore, R. F. (2016). "Getting to scale . . ." it seemed like a good idea at the time. *Journal of Educational Change, 17*(4), 529–537.

Firestone, W. A., & Wilson, B. L. (1985). Using bureaucratic and cultural linkages to improve instruction: The principal's contribution. *Educational Administration Quarterly, 21*(2), 7–30.

Frayer, D., Frederick, W. C., & Klausmeier, H. J. (1969). *A schema for testing the level of cognitive mastery.* Madison, WI: Wisconsin Center for Education Research.

Friziellie, H., Schmidt, J. A., & Spiller, J. (2016). *Yes we can! General and special educators collaborating in a professional learning community.* Bloomington, IN: Solution Tree Press.

Gallimore, R., Ermeling, B. A., Saunders, W. M., & Goldenberg, C. (2009). Moving the learning of teaching closer to practice: Teacher education implications of school-based inquiry teams. *Elementary School Journal, 109*(5), 537–553.

Gladwell, M. (2002). *The tipping point: How little things can make a big difference.* Boston: Back Bay Books.

Hansen, A. (2015). *How to develop PLCs for singletons and small schools.* Bloomington, IN: Solution Tree Press.

Hattie, J. (2009). *Visible learning: A synthesis of over 800 meta-analyses relating to achievement.* New York: Routledge.

Hattie, J. (2016). *Collective teacher efficacy according to John Hattie.* Accessed at https://visible-learning.org/2018/03/collective-teacher-efficacy-hattie on June 23, 2019.

Hirsch, J. (2017, July 6). *3 ways to build trust on your team* [Blog post]. Accessed at https://leadx.org/articles/trust on April 4, 2019.

Huberman, M. (1993). The model of the independent artisan in teachers' professional relations. In J. W. Little & M. Wallin McLaughlin (Eds.), *Teachers work: Individuals, colleagues, and contexts* (pp. 11–50). New York: Teachers College Press.

Kanold, T. D. (2011). *The five disciplines of PLC leaders.* Bloomington, IN: Solution Tree Press.

Kanter, R. M. (2006). *Confidence: How winning streaks and losing streaks begin and end.* New York: Three Rivers Press.

Kelly, L. (2013, February 21). *The change process* [Blog post]. Accessed at www .rebelsatwork.com/blog/2013/02/21/the-change-process?rq=lois%2Bkelly on April 10, 2019.

Kelly, L. (2016, March 29). *Build these three change muscles* [Blog post]. Accessed at www.rebelsatwork.com/blog/2016/03/29/build-these-three-change-muscles ?rq=change%2Bmuscles on April 10, 2019.

Killian, S. (2017, September 24). *Hattie's 2017 updated list of factors influencing student achievement.* Accessed at www.evidencebasedteaching.org.au/hatties-2017-updated -list on April 10, 2019.

Kotter, J. P., & Cohen, D. S. (2002). *The heart of change: Real-life stories of how people change their organizations.* Boston: Harvard Business Review Press.

Kramer, S. V., & Schuhl, S. (2017). *School improvement for all: A how-to guide for doing the right work.* Bloomington, IN: Solution Tree Press.

Lencioni, P. (2002). *The five dysfunctions of a team.* San Francisco: Jossey-Bass.

Levi, D. (2011). *Group dynamics for teams* (3rd ed.). Thousand Oaks, CA: SAGE.

Levi, D. (2017). *Group dynamics for teams* (5th ed.). Los Angeles: SAGE.

Marzano, R. J. (2010). *The art and science of teaching: A comprehensive framework for effective instruction.* Alexandria, VA: Association for Supervision and Curriculum Development.

Mattos, M. (2014). *Are we a group or a team? Moving from coordination to collaboration in a PLC at Work.* Bloomington, IN: Solution Tree Press.

Mattos, M., & Buffum, A. (Eds.). (2014). *It's about time: Planning interventions and extensions in secondary school.* Bloomington, IN: Solution Tree Press.

Mattos, M., DuFour, R., DuFour, R., Eaker, R., & Many, T. W. (2016). *Concise answers to frequently asked questions about Professional Learning Communities at Work.* Bloomington, IN: Solution Tree Press.

Meadows, D. H. (2008). *Thinking in systems: A primer.* D. Wright (Ed.). White River Junction, VT: Chelsea Green.

Mehrabian, A. (1981). *Silent messages: Implicit communication of emotions and attitudes.* Belmont, CA: Wadsworth.

Merrow, J. (2017). *Addicted to reform: A 12-step program to rescue public education.* New York: The New Press.

Miller, R., & Rowan, B. (2006). Effects of organic management on student achievement. *American Educational Research Journal, 43*(2), 219–253.

Muhammad, A. (2017). *Transforming school culture: How to overcome staff division* (2nd ed.). Bloomington, IN: Solution Tree Press.

National Governors Association Center for Best Practices & Council of Chief State School Officers. (2010). *Common Core State Standards for English language arts and literacy in history/social studies, science, and technical subjects*. Washington, DC: Authors. Accessed at www.corestandards.org/assets/CCSSI_ELA%20Standards.pdf on March 27, 2019.

Newmann, F. (1996). *Authentic achievement: Restructuring schools for intellectual quality*. San Francisco: Jossey-Bass.

O'Neill, J., & Conzemius, A. E. (2013). *The handbook for SMART school teams: Revitalizing best practices for collaboration* (2nd ed.). Bloomington, IN: Solution Tree Press.

Patterson, K., Grenny, J., Maxfield, D., McMillan, R., & Switzler, A. (2008). *Influencer: The power to change anything*. New York: McGraw-Hill.

Patterson, K., Grenny, J., McMillan, R., & Switzler, A. (2002). *Crucial conversations: Tools for talking when stakes are high*. New York: McGraw-Hill Education.

Perkins, D. (2003). *King Arthur's round table: How collaborative conversations create smart organizations*. Hoboken, NJ: John Wiley & Sons.

Peterson, K. D., & Deal, T. E. (1998). How leaders influence the culture of schools. *Educational Leadership*, *56*(1), 28–30.

Rath, T., & Conchie, B. (2008). *Strengths based leadership: Great leaders, teams, and why people follow*. New York: Gallup Press.

Reeves, D. (2002). *The leader's guide to standards: A blueprint for educational equity and excellence*. San Francisco: Jossey-Bass.

Reeves, D., & DuFour, R. (2016). The futility of PLC lite. *Phi Delta Kappan*, *97*(6), 69–71.

Ross, J. A., Hogaboam-Gray, A., & Gray, P. (2004). Prior student achievement, collaborative school processes, and collective teacher efficacy. *Leadership and Policy in Schools*, *3*(3), 163–188.

Saunders, W., Goldenberg, C., & Gallimore, R. (2009). Increasing achievement by focusing grade-level teams on improving classroom learning: A prospective, quasi-experimental study of Title I schools. *American Educational Research Journal*, *46*(4), 1006–1033. Accessed at www.jstor.org/stable/40284745 on June 24, 2016.

Schmoker, M. (2004). Tipping point: From feckless reform to substantive instructional improvement. *Phi Delta Kappan*, *85*(6), 424–432.

Schmoker, M. (2018). *Focus: Elevating the essentials to radically improve student learning* (2nd ed.). Alexandria, VA: Association for Supervision and Curriculum Development.

Skloot, R. (2011). *The immortal life of Henrietta Lacks*. New York: Random House.

Smith, F., Mihalakis, V., & Slamp, A. (2016). *4 ways that leadership teams create conditions for success in schools* [Blog post]. Accessed at http://k12education .gatesfoundation.org/blog/school-leadership-teams-create-conditions-success-in -schools on April 10, 2019.

Stolp, S., & Smith, S. C. (1995). *Transforming school culture: Stories, symbols, values, and the leader's role.* Eugene, OR: ERIC Clearinghouse on Educational Management.

Stuart, T. S. (Ed.). (2016). *Global perspectives: Professional Learning Communities at Work in international schools.* Bloomington, IN: Solution Tree Press.

Thompson, C. (2013, November 12). *Coblaboration vs. collaboration* [Blog post]. Accessed at http://regionalphysics.blogspot.com/2013/11/coblaboration-vs -collaboration-for.html on April 10, 2019.

Tucker, M. (2015). Needed: An updated accountability model. *Educational Leadership,* *72*(5), 66–70.

Tuckman, B. W. (1965). Developmental sequence in small groups. *Psychological Bulletin, 63*(6), 384–399.

Vescio, V., Ross, D., & Adams, A. (2008). A review of research on the impact of professional learning communities on teaching practice and student learning. *Teaching and Teacher Education: An International Journal of Research and Studies, 24*(1), 80–91.

Weigle, B. (n.d.). Why your testing attitude affects student results [Blog post]. *Classroom Caboodle.* Accessed at https://classroomcaboodle.com/teacher-resource /testing-attitude-affects-results on March 28, 2019.

Windram, H., Bollman, K., & Johnson, S. (2012). *How RTI works in secondary schools: Building a framework for success.* Bloomington, IN: Solution Tree Press.

Wooden, J., & Jamison, S. (2005). *Wooden on leadership: How to create a winning organization.* New York: McGraw-Hill Education.

Index